ESSENTIALS OF

Critical-Constructivist
Grounded Theory Research

Essentials of Qualitative Methods Series

ESSENTIALS OF

Critical-Constructivist Grounded Theory Research

Heidi M. Levitt

 AMERICAN PSYCHOLOGICAL ASSOCIATION

Published by
American Psychological Association
750 First Street, NE
Washington, DC 20002
https://www.apa.org

Order Department
https://www.apa.org/pubs/books
order@apa.org

In the U.K., Europe, Africa, and the Middle East, copies may be ordered from Eurospan
https://www.eurospanbookstore.com/apa
info@eurospangroup.com

Typeset in Charter and Interstate by Circle Graphics, Inc., Reisterstown, MD

Printer: Sheridan Books, Chelsea, MI
Cover Designer: Anne C. Kerns, Anne Likes Red, Inc., Silver Spring, MD

Library of Congress Cataloging-in-Publication Data

Names: Levitt, Heidi M., author.
Title: Essentials of critical-constructivist grounded theory research /
  by Heidi M. Levitt.
Description: Washington, DC : American Psychological Association, [2021] |
  Series: Essentials of qualitative methods series | Includes bibliographical
  references and index.
Identifiers: LCCN 2020041290 (print) | LCCN 2020041291 (ebook) |
  ISBN 9781433834523 (paperback) | ISBN 9781433836763 (ebook)
Subjects: LCSH: Grounded theory. | Qualitative research—Methodology. |
  Psychology—Qualitative research. | Critical theory. | Constructivism (Psychology)
Classification: LCC H61.24 .L37 2021 (print) | LCC H61.24 (ebook) |
  DDC 001.4/2—dc23
LC record available at https://lccn.loc.gov/2020041290
LC ebook record available at https://lccn.loc.gov/2020041291

https://doi.org/10.1037/0000231-000

Printed in the United States of America

10 9 8 7 6 5 4 3 2 1

Contents

Series Foreword

Qualitative approaches have become accepted and indeed embraced as empirical methods within the social sciences, as scholars have realized that many of the phenomena in which we are interested are complex and require deep inner reflection and equally penetrating examination. Quantitative approaches often cannot capture such phenomena well through their standard methods (e.g., self-report measures), so qualitative designs using interviews and other in-depth data-gathering procedures offer exciting, nimble, and useful research approaches.

Indeed, the number and variety of qualitative approaches that have been developed is remarkable. We remember Bill Stiles saying (quoting Chairman Mao) at one meeting about methods, "Let a hundred flowers bloom," indicating that there are many appropriate methods for addressing research questions. In this series, we celebrate this diversity (hence, the cover design of flowers).

The question for many of us, though, has been how to decide among approaches and how to learn the different methods. Many prior descriptions of the various qualitative methods have not provided clear enough descriptions of the methods, making it difficult for novice researchers to learn how to use them. Thus, those interested in learning about and pursuing qualitative research need crisp and thorough descriptions of these approaches, with lots of examples to illustrate the method so that readers can grasp how to use the methods.

The purpose of this series of books, then, is to present a range of different qualitative approaches that seemed most exciting and illustrative of the range of methods appropriate for social science research. We asked leading experts in qualitative methods to contribute to the series, and we were delighted that they accepted our invitation. Through this series, readers have the opportunity to learn qualitative research methods from those who developed the methods and/or who have been using them successfully for years.

We asked the authors of each book to provide context for the method, including a rationale, situating the method within the qualitative tradition, describing the method's philosophical and epistemological background, and noting the key features of the method. We then asked them to describe in detail the steps of the method, including the research team, sampling, biases and expectations, data collection, data analysis, and variations on the method. We also asked authors to provide tips for the research process and for writing a manuscript emerging from a study that used the method. Finally, we asked authors to reflect on the methodological integrity of the approach, along with the benefits and limitations of the particular method.

This series of books can be used in several different ways. Instructors teaching courses in qualitative research could use the whole series, presenting one method at a time to expose students to a range of qualitative methods. Alternatively, instructors could choose to focus on just a few approaches, as depicted in specific books, supplementing the books with examples from studies that have been published using the approaches, and providing experiential exercises to help students get started using the approaches.

In this book, Heidi M. Levitt presents grounded theory from a critical-constructivist perspective. Grounded theory is one of the earliest formalized qualitative methods (Glaser & Strauss, 1967) and is quite popular among researchers in the social sciences. Levitt presents grounded theory as a flexible method that can be adapted to a study's particular emphases and characteristics. She uses examples from her own extensive research experience to demonstrate the main tenets of grounded theory (i.e., constant comparison, development of a hierarchy, theoretical sampling, saturation, and memoing) and to support grounded theory's methodological integrity. Levitt astutely describes both the benefits and limitations of the method and offers a useful timeline to help those considering a grounded theory project anticipate the tempo and demands of such research.

—*Clara E. Hill and Sarah Knox*

ESSENTIALS OF

Critical-Constructivist
Grounded Theory Research

1 CONCEPTUAL FOUNDATIONS OF CRITICAL-CONSTRUCTIVIST GROUNDED THEORY

When I was a graduate student at York University during the 1990s, qualitative methods were being advanced at a time when they still were rare in most psychology programs (see Rennie, 2010, for a description of this innovative program's history). Beginning graduate school, I had wanted to become a therapist and to use constructivist, artistic, and integrative approaches to help my clients make meaning of their experiences. It was only through the process of learning about qualitative methods that I decided to make research a central aspect of my career.

The qualitative method I first learned was grounded theory (Glaser & Strauss, 1967), popularized in psychology (and introduced to me) by one of my mentors, David Rennie (e.g., Rennie et al., 1988). Although qualitative inquiry has been used in psychology since its beginning (e.g., in Freud, 1900, and Maslow's, 1968, work; Wertz, 2014), grounded theory was one of the earliest formalized qualitative methods in psychology. By this, I mean it is a method laid out intentionally with clear steps for researchers to follow.

Being curious about new approaches to research, I wanted to try out this method myself. I used it in my first independent research project as a graduate student, when I interviewed Tibetan-Buddhist monks living in

https://doi.org/10.1037/0000231-001
Essentials of Critical-Constructivist Grounded Theory Research, by H. M. Levitt

Dharmsala, India, about the development of wisdom (Levitt, 1999). I was humbled to be welcomed into the monastery to conduct interviews and learn about their tradition. One of my favorite research memories still is of drinking hot butter and salt tea in their library and discussing wisdom with rhythmic chanting prayers resonating in the background. In my dissertation project, I used this approach again in a mixed-methods study, interviewing clients about their experiences of silence and developing a process measure to distinguish experiences of silence (e.g., Levitt, 2001). I was especially intrigued to learn about the many experiences in therapy that clients do not share with their therapists. After these experiences, I thought to myself, What could be better than having a job in which you get to listen to people's experiences about the very topics that you find most fascinating? What could be better than being able to dialogue with people who know more than you do about the topics that you wish to understand? As a qualitative researcher, I would gain the credentials to ask questions, develop my thinking, and share ideas with others. The role of a qualitative researcher offered an inside window into the internal experiences of others and the mysteries therein. It allowed me to question my assumptions and expand my horizons. I was hooked. I hope this book supports you in learning more about the issues and questions that most intrigue you and that you experience a similar excitement and growth.

Since that time, qualitative research has become integrated into psychological methods to the extent that would have been hard for my younger self to imagine. Division 5 of the American Psychological Association (APA), which focuses on methods, has shifted its name to Quantitative and Qualitative Psychology, and their section, the Society for Qualitative Inquiry in Psychology (SQIP), is thriving with annual conferences and its own journal. In the British Psychological Society, the section Qualitative Methods in Psychology was formed in 2005 (Madill, 2015) and since has become the largest section in the organization. An SQIP task force of qualitative researchers who use a wide range of methods has developed guidelines for designing and evaluating qualitative research to guide reviewers in unique aspects of qualitative research (Levitt, Motulsky, et al., 2017). Qualitative research is being published now in journals that used to be limited to quantitative methods, and their use is increasing (Gough & Lyons, 2016). Also, standards for reporting qualitative research have become integrated into APA Style and the *Publication Manual of the American Psychological Association* (APA, 2020; Levitt et al., 2018), influencing criteria for publishing across the social sciences.

As one of the earliest qualitative methods in psychology, grounded theory has become one of the most commonly used qualitative methods in psychological research, with a diversity of approaches to this method being put forward.

Through this book, I draw on my research experience as well as a broad base of research in the field to exemplify this method. At this point, I have been using grounded theory for over 20 years, and my approach has evolved into the version I present in this book.

In this chapter, I first describe what grounded theory is and then how it has been used within a range of epistemological perspectives, to contextualize my critical-constructivist approach. To be clear at the outset about my own perspective, I am not an advocate of the uniform adoption of my approach to grounded theory or even qualitative methods. I am a mixed-methods researcher who uses both qualitative and quantitative methods in her programs of research. Fundamentally, I believe in using whatever methods that will advance your inquiry, given your goals and the characteristics of your study, and you will see this theme running across this book. Learning about methods provides you with tools and, by understanding their unique strengths, you can choose the best approach to answering your question. I present my approach to grounded theory to guide you in considering which procedures fit for you and to support you in tailoring grounded theory methods to suit your purposes.

WHAT IS GROUNDED THEORY?

Grounded theory was developed by sociologists Barney Glaser and Anselm Strauss (1967), who were looking to formalize a methodological approach through which theory could be developed from the analysis of data. They argued that the act of verifying theories had become primary in sociology and that the scientific function of generating theory had become secondary but should be recentralized. A strong grounded theory "fits empirical situations, and is understandable to sociologists and layman alike. Most important, it works—provides us with relevant predictions, explanations, interpretations and applications" (Glaser & Strauss, 1967, p. 1). They sought to systematize the discovery of theory so that it evolved thorough close observation of data and would be useful for this range of functions.

A central function of this approach is to forestall researchers from grasping too quickly on a theory—that is, the set of ideas designed to explain the phenomenon under study. There are a number of dangers related to doing so. Researchers might seek to use an existing theory that does not fit the data as well as it could, especially because of the field's orientation toward the verification of existing theories. Or they might seek out examples that support the theories that they have found helpful and not look to disconfirm or problematize their beliefs as they investigate new issues or groups of people. As certain theories become popular, they may overshadow alternative ways of understanding phenomena. In contrast, grounded theory researchers are guided to develop new understandings through the cumulative study of data. They continue to evolve the theory in relation to continued observation until they are confident that the theory holds and can provide a useful answer to their research question.

This method became a classic approach to qualitative inquiry because the proposal herein was a radical challenge to the understanding of how science was practiced. Previously, there was little guidance for the act of developing theory, and often theory development was seen as comparable to guesswork. There was little knowledge on how to develop empirically-based hypotheses for quantitative studies or psychological models. In contrast, Glaser and Strauss (1967) set out to develop a new set of procedures that was appropriate for building theory. They argued that theory should be empirically driven and based on a process of systematic observation. They saw both qualitative and quantitative methods as useful to develop and verify theory and thought that both forms of analysis are often necessary. Qualitative research, and grounded theory specifically, were seen as particularly helpful in forming theory about topics that are complex, influenced by structural factors, characterized by social norms, and located within interpersonal systems. For these same reasons, grounded theory has been widely adopted in many spheres of psychological study, including educational (Sutcliffe, 2016), developmental (e.g., Budge et al., 2018), organizational (Carrero et al., 2000), clinical (e.g., Oddli & Rønnestad, 2012), counseling (e.g., Arczynski & Morrow, 2017), cultural (e.g., Bowleg, 2004), and medical research (e.g., Granek et al., 2019).

In psychology, grounded theory most often is used to develop an empirically driven understanding of a phenomenon—and less often resulting in a grand theory (Charmaz, 2008). Grounded theory methods are used most often to develop detailed descriptions and explanations of lived experiences that are intended to be applied within a certain context. These findings can be taken as a basis for theory, hypothesis testing, and application in a wide variety of ways, however, and so they serve a similar function as theory even when they are framed in a more localized manner. This framing may reflect the movement toward constructivist approaches in psychology that value situated knowledge to facilitate its application, as is described more in the section on epistemology in this chapter. As a consequence, while the results of these analyses are often described as theories, this term should be understood loosely.

It is important to make clear, though, that these studies also can provide the groundwork for the development of a formal theory (Glaser, 2013). For

instance, David Rennie's (2007) classic study on psychotherapy clients' experience produced the theory that radical reflexivity is the central activity of
therapy. This theory has broad implications for the practice of therapy by
focusing therapists on the importance of supporting client agency in sessions.
Although the purposes for grounded theory have diversified, individual studies
also can lead to grand theories via meta-analyses and research reviews.

GROUNDED THEORY AS SITUATED IN QUALITATIVE RESEARCH

Knowing a variety of methods can allow you to select those that will best
advance your goals. Across every qualitative method, it is my experience that
an investigator's depth of knowledge of a phenomenon, devotion to careful
analysis, and analytic abilities are pivotal. At the same time, specific methods
can support researchers to develop findings that take a certain form and have
potential uses. In the next sections, I provide a quick overview of this approach
and then shift to explain the most common reasons for using a grounded
theory approach to help you consider why this approach might distinctively
benefit your program of study.

Why Select Grounded Theory Methods? How Do They Work?

Grounded theory methods most often are used to guide researchers to conceptualize an internal experience and/or to understand how a practice takes shape
interpersonally and/or across a larger system. At heart, these approaches are
based in a cycle of inferences that is centered on induction, meaning that they
do not begin with a set of categories to be used for coding, but they develop
categories from the close analysis of data (Glaser & Strauss, 1967)—hence
they are "grounded." Grounded theory methods can be used with a wide
range of data, including texts, social media posts, speeches, observational
notes, and conversations. In psychology, they tend to be used most often to
analyze semistructured interviews of participants that contain a rich description of an experience. Consequently, this is the kind of data I emphasize most
often in this book, but it can translate easily to the data you are studying.
If the data contain detailed descriptions of the phenomenon you are studying,
the method will work well.

Here, I quickly summarize some central processes in this approach so
you have a sense of the process of analysis (a detailed description is provided
throughout the book). Grounded theory methods work by guiding researchers
to segment their data into units and then to assign a label to each unit. Next,
researchers compare each of the units with one another and group them into

initial categories on the basis of the patterns identified therein. Then, the researchers examine the categories that they created and compare them in turn, grouping them into higher order categories. The higher order categories are examined next in this same way, and this process continues until researchers develop a hierarchy of categories. At the top of the hierarchy is a core category that articulates the theory that has emerged from the analytic process. Because of this organization of data into a hierarchy, researchers usually select grounded theory as their qualitative method of choice because they wish to develop a conceptualization of the phenomenon that is grounded in the experiences reported, with subcategories that identify the components of that theory or description. I like teaching grounded theory methods because they support novice qualitative researchers in engaging in this conceptual work by moving step by step—from the data to units, to initial categories, and to higher level categories. The hierarchical structure gives researchers confidence in describing how their central findings emerged because they can point to the categories beneath that led to their composition. There are a number of additional ways this structure can be helpful, and the next section reviews these strengths of the method.

Ways Grounded Theory Findings Benefit a Program of Research

When researchers select a qualitative method, they consider not only the form of results that might be useful for that one study but also how the results would benefit their continued program of research. In this section, I describe when the results from a grounded theory analysis can be distinctly helpful within your larger program of research.

Mixed Methods

Grounded theory methods can be used in mixed-methods approaches to research in which qualitative and quantitative methods are combined either sequentially or concurrently. How findings from quantitative analyses take shape in people's lived experiences can be better understood when followed with this qualitative analysis. Also, grounded theory research can lead to the identification and refinement of hypotheses for future quantitative research. Given the amount of resources that go into quantitative research, I always prefer to begin programs of research with a qualitative study so I am confident that my hypotheses make sense for my specific population and that they would be invested in my research because of its utility to them. Although this text does not focus on mixed-methods research, there are guides available in varied disciplines (e.g., Creswell, 2009; Lindlof & Taylor, 2017).

Developing Measures

The development of a hierarchy has particular application for the future development of measures. I often think of the process of organizing a hierarchy as being akin to factor analysis because you are grouping together ideas that you think are most tightly interconnected. Higher order categories can suggest factors to be tested quantitatively. Initial categories can suggest items to be evaluated. The detailed nature of the hierarchy can be helpful when developing both process measures to be applied when coding transcripts as well as outcome measures to assess treatments. The hierarchy provides a convincing rationale for the categories and factors within each measure, showing how they evolved from the reported experiences of clients. If you are considering the development of a measure as an outcome of your research, grounded theory methods may be especially useful for your project.

Developing Treatment Strategies, Policy Recommendations, and Curricula

Because of the generation of a hierarchy with multiple levels of categories, a grounded theory analysis can support the formation of comprehensive and detailed recommendations for education, policy, and clinical care. By identifying the major causes for concern or the central sites where attention is needed, researchers can be guided to consider how to address an issue across systems (e.g., Auerbach et al., 2006). The construction of a hierarchy can assist with the detailing of the problems, situations, and possible remedies that can be considered within program development. For instance, you might find that an intervention for a health problem (e.g., HIV) is needed at the level of health education, practitioner training, and public media. Subcategories within separate arms of the hierarchy can indicate the best way to approach each pathway (e.g., identifying messages to be addressed in sessions, regulations, or modules). The goals at the outset of your study can guide you to provide detailed answers and a multifaceted response.

In addition, in Chapter 5, I discuss the use of grounded theory methods in meta-analyses to create formal theories based on a field of research. In Chapter 2, specific types of questions that are recommended, or contraindicated, for this approach are described in greater depth.

EPISTEMOLOGICAL PERSPECTIVES

Before discussing grounded theory methods, I describe the role of epistemological perspectives and their influence (for a primer on philosophical perspectives on qualitative methods, see Ponterotto, 2005). When qualitative researchers describe their *epistemological assumptions*, they communicate their theory of knowledge and the processes that they feel enhance knowledge production. For instance, do they see it as located within an external reality, interpersonal interactions, or social systems? Do they see the act of knowing as driven by observation, interpretation, or theory? Understanding these traditions can help you to select an approach and understand the research of others.

Researcher epistemologies have been organized in many ways (e.g., Guba & Lincoln, 2005; Levitt, Motulsky, et al., 2017; Ponterotto, 2005), but three central epistemological perspectives include postpositivist, constructivist, and critical perspectives. Before discussing these approaches, though, it should be made clear that not all qualitative researchers explicate an epistemological approach. *Pragmatic* researchers are not bound to any one epistemological approach but use varying methods to achieve practical goals and solve problems (Fishman & Westerman, 2011; Patton, 2015). They may move between methods, procedures, and epistemic approaches to further their goals. Also, psychologists might endorse multiple perspectives (e.g., having a critical-constructivist approach) or vary their approach to suit their project aims. Over time, the approach to inquiry that the originators of grounded theory method put forward has been questioned (by themselves, as well as others), resulting in the propagation of multiple versions of grounded theory that are based in distinctive traditions of inquiry and sets of procedures (e.g., Bryant & Charmaz, 2013; Rennie, 2012). Central approaches are described here.

Postpositivist Foundations

Postpositivist researchers espouse the goal of using objective approaches to analysis toward generating reliable explanations or predictions. They are concerned about reducing human error and biases as much as possible to closely approximate an external reality under study that can be observed and agreed on (i.e., a realist view). As problems with the measurement of psychological phenomena arose, however, researchers adopted a postpositivist perspective, which sought to overcome problems of measurement and bias by using better tools and measures while still viewing the credibility of methods as resting on claims of objectivity and seeking the replicability of study findings (Levitt, Surace, et al., in press). In qualitative psychology, it appears that the postpositivist approach to qualitative research is waning and that constructivist perspectives are dominant, with critical approaches becoming more prevalent (Levitt, Pomerville, et al., 2017).

Grounded theory method was developed in the 1960s in a period during which qualitative researchers were seeking responses to criticism from their postpositivist quantitative peers about the validity of their methods (Bryant

& Charmaz, 2013). Grounded theory developed, in part, as an argument to defend qualitative practices to researchers who held realist beliefs about what scientific practices are valuable (e.g., objectivity, bias reduction). Glaser and Strauss (1967) wished to advance these approaches by developing a systematic method of qualitative research that would make coherent processes often invisible in qualitative analyses. In pursuing these goals, grounded theory was first articulated in what appeared to be objectivist rhetoric to appeal to many sociologists of that era, emphasizing the discovery (vs. construction) of theory and using language implying uncomplicated access to external reality. Current postpositivist grounded theory researchers (e.g., Kempster & Parry, 2011; Lo, 2014) tend to incorporate procedures to demonstrate objectivity and reliability, such as evaluating hypotheses within their process of coding (Strauss & Corbin, 1990), assessing interrater reliability, or using methods to demonstrate that the researchers were objective within the analytic process.

Constructivist Foundations

Constructivist researchers examine their dialogue to learn about the meanings held by their participants and their interpersonal systems. Grounded theory method was reflective of the Chicago School's pragmatic philosophy, George Herbert Mead's symbolic interactionism, and ethnographic traditions that all were concerned with the social basis of meaning and so appealed to constructivists (Bryant & Charmaz, 2013). They are interested in how meaning is constructed interpersonally, identifying both those processes and the meanings themselves to develop a deeper understanding of a phenomenon. Internal meanings are thought to be unfolding within a particular social context that needs to be explicated from the point of view of the participant (Jeon, 2004).

Notable constructivist approaches to grounded theory were developed and popularized in psychology by Kathy Charmaz (2014) and David Rennie (2000). In contrast to postpositivists, they hold that there can be multiple valid versions of reality, and they illustrate in their analyses the social process of developing meaning. These approaches often take the form of examining the interpretive lenses through which an analysis takes place, revealing the assumptions, needs, and traditions of a group. For instance, for a mother of a child with cancer, the meaning of motherhood has unique aspects. Developing an understanding of how women maintain identities that are both sites of pain and happiness can facilitate supports for mothers in this difficult position (e.g., McEvoy, 2019). Constructivist grounded theory researchers also tend to examine how researchers and participants co-construct meanings. They might examine how the phrasing or ordering of questions evolved as the understanding of a topic deepened.

Critical Foundations

Critical researchers engage in inquiry to promote liberation, transformation, consciousness raising, and social change. This approach can be understood as tied to grounded theory from the start because of its originators' interest in societal power dynamics (Bryant & Charmaz, 2013), and supplemental approaches such as situational analysis (Clarke, 2003) have been developed to support the integration of these aims. Although it is beyond the scope of this book to provide a thorough history of critical psychology or describe its many instantiations (see Fox & Prilleltensky, 1997; Parker, 2015; Teo, 2015), a brief description provides a frame for discussing critical methods.

Critical psychological theories have been characterized by a view of subjectivity as embedded in society and as intrinsically influenced by cultural, contextual, and historical forces related to social power and oppression. With this perspective, grounded theory researchers used their methods to analyze how sociopolitical structures and processes support the privilege of dominant classes in society (e.g., gender, race, ethnicity, sexual orientation, immigration status; Allen, 2011; Steinberg & Cannella, 2012). These researchers shed light on otherwise invisible forces of oppression and injustice that have become the status quo and seek to generate emancipatory social change (e.g., Fine, 2013). They critique the ways our discipline engages in acts that might perpetuate discriminatory practices and perspectives.

Although critical qualitative researchers tend to centralize varied theories of systemic oppression, using perspectives such as critical race theory (e.g., Bowleg, 2004), critical queer theory (e.g., Diamond, 2006), disability theory (e.g., Kafer, 2013), postcolonial theory (e.g., Gone, 2019), feminist approaches to sexuality (e.g., Tiefer, 2018), and Marxist theory (e.g., Roberts, 2014) to draw attention to varied and/or intersecting forms of societal power within and without psychology, commonalities in their methods have been noted. Like constructivist approaches, these methods also are centered on the recognition that the research process is invariably influenced by the perspectives of the researcher, from the conception of a research question to the ways data are collected, analyses are conducted, findings are written, and applications of findings are developed (Teo, 2015). Because critical researchers are aware that their views are limited by their perspectives and social situations, they have generated procedures to assist them in conducting research that is grounded in the lived experience and knowledge of people who have experienced the forms of oppression under study (Fine, 2016). Critical participatory methods may engage an advisory team from the group under study, recruit coresearchers from that group, and engage participants to guide the development of the research question, research design, data collection, analysis, and/or application of findings (e.g., Fine, 2013; Gone, 2019). For instance, grounded theory researchers might examine how ethnocentrism influences the perception of cross-racial psychotherapy (e.g., Chang & Yoon, 2011). Critical epistemological perspectives are defined by their distinct goals that center on developing knowledge to advance social justice, institutional change, and empowerment.

CRITICAL-CONSTRUCTIVIST GROUNDED THEORY

It might be because of the ambiguity of its philosophical premises that grounded theory methods were embraced so widely across psychology. They spoke to researchers of quite different ilks. There is such diversity in the ways that grounded theory is used that Fassinger (2005) described it as "a paradigmatic bridge between postpositivist, interpretive/constructivist, and poststructural or critical approaches to qualitative research" (p. 157). She described how this flexibility has allowed researchers who are comfortable with experimentalist methods to adopt qualitative methods while retaining their beliefs in the value of verification of theory. At the same time, researchers who see knowledge as interpersonally constructed or as structured by social forces also may find grounded theory to be congenial when examining research questions addressing interpersonal and societal problems. Indeed, Rennie (2000) described grounded theory as a merging of relativism, as findings were developed within researchers' interpretations, and of realism, as their interpretations had to hold true to the empirical data to be credible. Many versions of grounded theory analysis have been put forward, some of which I discuss to contextualize this approach, although it is not possible for me to review all their differences in this slim textbook. It is important to note, however, that aspects of grounded theory method have been tied to more than one approach to inquiry (Age, 2011), so investigators often describe their epistemological perspectives as characterized by the beliefs about inquiry that make clear their motives for and process of engaging in research. In that vein, I describe critical-constructivist grounded theory.

In this book, I extend an approach to grounded theory that is based on a constructivist version developed by David Rennie (2000) and that I see as compatible with both versions of constructivist grounded theory and critical and feminist grounded theory methods (e.g., Allen, 2011; Charmaz, 2014; Gibson, 2013; Olsen, 2013). I situate this approach within the critical and constructivist epistemological traditions, described in the prior sections, because I find that these approaches are especially appropriate for studying questions that relate to psychosocial experience. I am influenced by philosophical theory that extends the meaning of causality to recognize how qualitative methods identify causal processes (e.g., Cartwright, 2007; Maxwell, 2012) and the potential for qualitative findings to both generalize and transfer across settings (Levitt, in press), although these are not a focus of the current text. Depending on your research question, you may want to emphasize the methods related to the constructivist or critical side of this approach, and I encourage you to use the procedures that seem useful to you.

This approach asks researchers to consider the experience or practice under study in relation to (a) how and why meanings are formed interpersonally; (b) how privilege, oppression, and systemic difference influence experiences; and (c) how the research context (and its power dynamics) shapes findings. Thinking about the construction and social situation of research topics can generate insight into their origins and modes of functioning. This book is focused on methods, rather than theory, and so does not review the many constructivist (e.g., Charmaz, 2008) and critical theories (e.g., Steinberg & Cannella, 2012) that can guide qualitative research. Instead, its focus is on providing guidance after you have selected the types of constructivist (e.g., social constructionist, symbolic interactionist, postmodern) or critical (e.g., feminist, queer, multicultural, economic) approaches that you are drawing on to further your research goals. It articulates the procedures that support the inquiry process across these theories and guides you to consider the rationale for their use in relation to your methods.

Because qualitative research in psychology often is used to investigate the holistic experience of a phenomenon or activity and examine cultural and systemic contexts, this approach seems most relevant to the contemporary concerns of psychology today. The degree to which I engage processes that are constructivist or critical will depend on the study questions at hand and the project aims. When my goals are to illuminate societal processes, the critical aspects are drawn out (e.g., my gender research), but when my goals are to provide guidance to therapists, the in-session dynamics of constructing meaning interpersonally may be centralized. And at other times, both of these goals might be at play (e.g., overcoming heterosexist experiences in therapy) and of equal importance. I describe in detail how this philosophical grounding influences study design in Chapter 2.

KEY PROCEDURES IN GROUNDED THEORY METHOD

Grounded theory has captured the imaginations of generations of researchers who have developed variants of this method, leading to some complexity in describing its features. This description is complicated all the more because the two founders of grounded theory (Glaser & Strauss, 1967) separated in their understandings and went on to develop their own versions of the method (e.g., Glaser, 1992; Strauss & Corbin, 1990), and then second wave grounded theorists developed their own approaches (e.g., Charmaz, 2014; Clarke, 2009; Rennie, 2000). Readers and reviewers of grounded theory research often fail to recognize that there are multiple approaches and may face confusion when reading and reviewing studies. Other writers have compared these approaches (e.g., Corbin, 1998; Heath & Cowley, 2004; Rennie, 1998), but before we discuss what is distinctive about critical-constructivist grounded theory, I want to describe briefly the processes common across most versions of grounded theory. Each of these is discussed in greater depth later in the book.

Despite the procedural and epistemic variations, grounded theory approaches tend to share a number of characteristic elements (Fassinger, 2005). Critical-constructivist grounded theory incorporates these features, and throughout the body of this text, I discuss in greater detail how you can best adapt them for your purposes. Indeed, many of the innovative procedures stemming from grounded theory have gained traction and are integrated routinely into other qualitative approaches to enhance their methodological integrity (Levitt, Pomerville, et al., 2017).

Theoretical Sampling

In grounded theory, data collection typically is guided by theoretical sampling methods. In this process, data are collected in iterative waves to recruit people who can shed light on the developing theory. Researchers begin by recruiting participants who bring diversity to the analysis in ways that might be expected to be relevant to the topic under study. As the theory develops, investigators identify gaps in their understanding and then deliberately seek out participants to flesh out their understanding in that area. These procedures have gained broad acceptance in the field and are now routinely cited across methods to describe how qualitative researchers selected participants for their studies.

The Constant Comparison Method

Grounded theory analysis is rooted in the analytic process of constant comparison (Glaser & Strauss, 1967). In this process, each unit of data is compared with every other unit to identify patterns that become the basis of categories. Labels are generated for each category that describe the common pattern therein. The labeled categories are compared with one another in turn, and higher order categories are generated. These are labeled in turn to reflect their shared meanings. This process continues until a hierarchy is formed that has at its apex a *core category*, which is the central finding of the analysis. This method ensures the thoroughness of an analysis and is concluded at the point of data saturation.

Saturation

The point of *saturation* occurs when the addition of new data no longer appears to generate new understandings in the analysis. The data under analysis confirm the existing categories rather than lead to novel insights because much of the variation in the experience under study has already been described by prior participants. When a study reaches saturation, it is an indication that the analysis is comprehensive and that data collection can be stopped.

Memoing

Researchers engage in memoing throughout the process of conducting a study. This memoing structures their reflexive self-awareness, provides a forum for theoretical reflection and development, helps them keep track of the rationale and steps in their analysis, and permits reflection on coding decisions. More detail on memoing is provided in Chapter 2.

2 DESIGNING THE STUDY

The stage of designing a study allows you to consider the steps that will lead you to develop the best answer to your question. In this chapter, I consider the types of research project questions that are appropriate for critical-constructivist grounded theory, the way to set up a research team, the types of data that are useful, and the selection and recruitment of participants, and I introduce the concept of methodological integrity.

APPROPRIATE RESEARCH GOALS FOR A CRITICAL-CONSTRUCTIVIST GROUNDED THEORY METHOD

For every qualitative method, there are research goals and questions that are not appropriate. Here, I describe the types of research questions that are most suitable for critical-constructivist grounded theory methods and those that are contraindicated. The focus is on developing overall project questions rather than the specific questions to be asked in an interview (discussed in Chapter 4) or theories used in the analysis (discussed in Chapter 5).

https://doi.org/10.1037/0000231-002
Essentials of Critical-Constructivist Grounded Theory Research, by H. M. Levitt

Forming Categorized Findings That Are Grounded in Your Data

Grounded theory methods are most often used in psychology to guide researchers to conceptualize an internal experience or a phenomenon. Depending on their approach to inquiry and their goals, researchers often see this process as the development of a theory, a description, or an interpretation. Typically, researchers who use this approach have a central question that drives their interest. They are curious to learn the meanings associated with that question and how those meanings are generated socially. Findings of grounded theory analyses can take the form of a set of categories or the development of a theory that is tied to this general question.

Your phenomenon might be a social practice, internal experience, behavior, or otherwise. For instance, you might ask about the experience of holding a certain identity (e.g., a vocational identity, cultural identity, diagnostic identity) or having a certain experience (e.g., a health ailment, unusual expertise, a painful experience). Subquestions might examine how that identity or experience differs across contexts, challenges and advantages that result from having that identity or experience, and what it is like to talk about that identity or experience. The subquestions are developed to illuminate the central question. Or you might produce an overarching theory of the meaning of an identity in a specific place or time. In contrast, if you were interested in developing distinctive answers to a set of unrelated questions (e.g., How can I better teach my students? How can I change the administration at my school? How can I better support school counselors?), grounded theory might not be the method of choice (perhaps thematic or content analysis would make more sense).

Developing a Map of the Components Within a Phenomenon

Researchers use grounded theory methods to map out the elements that undergird an experience. Those elements can be conceptualized in a manner that makes sense in relation to your specific research question. For instance, you might be interested in learning about the types of microaggressions that occur within psychotherapy (Shelton & Delgado-Romero, 2013), about stages of personal development (Rihacek & Danelova, 2016), or about nuances in an interpersonal interaction (Arczynski & Morrow, 2017). As noted in Chapter 1, the hierarchy of categories structures findings so that they can effectively produce answers to varied questions.

Conceptualizing a Phenomenon Across Personal and Societal Levels

Grounded theory can encompass a wide variety of analytic processes. Initially, the process of grounded theory entails closely attending to the experience of the participants (from reading transcribed interviews or other data sources) and labeling the aspects of those experiences that illuminate the research question while remaining close to the participants' ideas and language. Later in the process of forming categories, the process of categorization becomes more abstract. We consider how the initial categories relate to higher processes of psychological functioning and societal systems then—emphasizing aspects that best fit our data and the project goals.

Using critical-constructivist grounded theory, you can consider both what is not spoken and what is implicit in the data, with an eye toward intrapersonal, interpersonal, and systemic dynamics. For instance, you can consider the discourses that are being used and how they are functioning to reproduce, resist, or challenge dominant ideas in the broader culture. Or you might find that the discourses reinforce, reproduce, or reinscribe dominant ideas. Even if participants or authors of texts are unaware of these dynamics, you can use critical theories to help you to notice these dynamics and challenge them (Fox & Prilleltensky, 1997; Steinberg & Cannella, 2012), and you can generate maps and diagrams to further your conceptualization of how people's identities and contexts are interrelated (Clarke, 2003). Integrating understandings from across personal and social perspectives of oppressive processes and ideological structures can stimulate creativity and innovation that can aid the development of a larger theory. For instance, in a study of the formation of friendships, the complexity of internal experience, social dynamics, and hegemonic structures may all influence those processes— thereby enriching your inquiry.

Developing a Conceptual Structure for Your Findings

The feature of grounded theory methods that is most distinguishing is the development of a hierarchical structure of categories that undergird a theory or set of findings. Indeed, the theory only emerges from developing initial categories that reflect common patterns of experiences observed in the data studied and then organizing them into higher order categories that reflect the patterns identified across the initial categories. Theory results from examining the systems of meaning and their use therein.

This process of developing such a conceptual structure is gratifying for several reasons. First, it enhances the researchers' confidence in their theory because they can see how it is grounded in the words and descriptions of their participants and data. Second, it allows researchers to more clearly articulate their theory and the components on which it rests. The hierarchy allows you to easily describe the foundations for conceptual elements within your theory that you can reference when questioned by committee members or journal reviewers. Your interpretive focus will guide the kind of conceptual structure that is developed. If your aim, data collection questions, and interpretive lens center on the construction of meaning, your hierarchy will reflect that. If these are centered on systemic features, your findings will reflect that. These can be integrated creatively.

The development of a theory from such a structure can be facilitated by thinking and reading about the conditions, actions, reactions, consequences, processes, and contexts associated with your phenomenon (e.g., Strauss & Corbin, 1990). You might deliberately think about each of these concepts in turn and how they relate to your data, or you might allow theory to emerge in relation to the questions of your research or the gaps you see in current theories in the literature. For instance, in developing a functionalist model of gender, my findings included functions of gender that were rooted in psychological, sociocultural, interpersonal, and sexual experiences (Levitt, 2019). The theory emerged in response to the problem that extant definitions of gender in psychology did not make sense for lesbian, gay, bisexual, transgender, and queer genders, and my finding that the only way I could develop an understanding of gender that remained cogent across the communities I studied was to consider its functions across these four domains. If your aim is to develop a theory from your analysis, it can be helpful to have this goal in mind throughout the project because it can guide you to ask questions that will illuminate the relationships that are relevant to your theoretical problem. Also, it will support bringing this sensitivity to your analysis. For more tips on the process of developing a theory, see Chapters 4 and 5.

CONTRAINDICATED QUESTIONS

There are times when grounded theory would not be a recommended method. The development of a detailed hierarchy is time intensive, and it is not useful for all purposes.

A Hierarchical Analysis Is Not Necessary

You may find that you can solve a research question that you have posed without needing to develop a hierarchical system of categories. For instance, you may wish to identify a single discourse theme to shift the way a topic is being framed in the media, and you might not find that multiple categories will be helpful. In contrast, you will find the effort of engaging in a labor-intensive grounded theory analysis most helpful when your goal is to develop a set of findings with clearly articulated components.

The Participants Are Unable to Provide the Rich Data Needed to Support a Hierarchical Analysis

There are a variety of reasons participants may not be able to provide the type of data that would enable a grounded theory analysis.

- Data collected already for an existing project might not contain the detail that would support a grounded theory analysis. For instance, if you are conducting a focus group in which participants described the kinds of cereal they most prefer, the data might not have the psychological depth that would make a grounded theory analysis worthwhile.

- When data are collected within a survey or online study, participants might be less likely to expand on their answers unless prompted to do so. If respondents have written only a sentence or two, it is less likely that the data would be fitting for the development of a data hierarchy.

- If the answer to your question lies outside of the participants' awareness (e.g., noticing how a psychoanalytic concept influences their therapy, commenting on an experience that they have not personally had), they may not be able to provide useful or detailed responses.

In general, you will find grounded theory to be most useful when you are studying a complex subject for which participants have been able to provide a rich description or which is described in detail in your data source.

The Aim of the Study Is Not to Develop an Organized Theory, Description, or Interpretation of a Phenomenon

Typically, grounded theory research is conducted to develop a singular hierarchically organized set of findings that results in a new understanding. Sometimes studies are conducted in which there are multiple closely related subfoci (e.g., the development, context, and enactment of resistance), which would make it more challenging to engage in a grounded theory study because it usually seeks to illuminate one unified theory from the data. Depending on your project goals, though, you may have a list of several distinct questions (e.g., if you are seeking to make sense of quantitative findings), and thus you may not be interested in developing a singular hierarchy or theoretical solution. Another method might then be better suited to those analyses (e.g., thematic or content analyses).

RESEARCH TEAM CONSIDERATIONS

Grounded theory methods can be used individually or within research teams of investigators. It would be an advantage to use a sole investigator when that author has a comprehensive knowledge of the data that could be compromised by a team. Their depth of understanding can lead them to make attuned interpretations and can provide a sensitivity to the issues raised by each participant. This strategy is especially helpful with complex topics.

When used within a team, an advantage is that the time entailed in conducting research can be divided among group members. Also, the varied lived experiences of researchers before entering the team can allow the data to be considered from multiple perspectives, potentially enriching the findings. Each strategy lacks the advantages of the other strategy, so it can be useful for researchers to consider what approach will best advantage their analysis. In addition, there are several considerations that I find helpful when working with a research team.

Discussing Your Perspectives Explicitly Through the Project

It can be helpful to begin projects with a discussion of the thoughts that a group has about a topic. This can begin right in the first meeting by having team members memo their thoughts and expectations and their concerns about how these might influence the project (Glaser & Strauss, 1967). One of the goals of considering the range of expectations held by a team is to help the group recognize that they will need to be cautious not to push their perspectives onto their participants or each other. Also, it is helpful to recognize that the readers of the research will hold diverse perspectives that likely will be even broader than those of the team, and so everyone's perspectives can help shape a project that can speak to a breadth of readers. It is helpful to revisit these ideas as group members' perspectives shift and are refined.

Considering Power Within the Team

It can help to address how power can influence the discourse within a team. For instance, professors who lead a research team may have the power to assign grades that can make team members reluctant to disagree with their perspectives. There may be team members who are from cultural backgrounds that are privileged within a setting or ones who are senior to others. Overt discussion that recognizes these differences, addresses fears, and encourages people to share their perspectives can help to empower the entire team (Hill, 2012). You may want to talk about this within your team periodically as well and consider the issues that are difficult to discuss together.

A Critical Consideration of Sources of Knowledge

In addition to considering the structural and unearned forms of power within a group, you may wish to consider which members have access to what form of knowledge. Feminist epistemologists have described this as *epistemic privilege* (Code, 1993; Harding, 2015). These theorists view people on the margins as having perspectives with special strengths due to their capacity to see the ways systems function by having experienced where they fail. This idea recently has been applied to considerations of how to manage consensus within qualitative research (Levitt, Ipecki, et al., 2020). For instance, in my teams, we discuss the unique perspectives and strengths that team members bring. The member who conducts an interview is assigned epistemological privilege because that person has the lived experience of the interview and access to nonverbal cues that the rest of the team lacks. That member is seen as a guide for interpreting that interview and as an advocate for the interviewee's perspective within the team—empowering interviewers to claim this authority and speak up if they think the group is misrepresenting the meanings in their interview.

Other forms of epistemological privilege can include lived experience and positionality (your life experiences may increase your sensitivity to interpret experiences in the data that are similar to your own), time investment (a team member who has spent much more time engaged in research might have a broader base for interpretation than a member with a surface engagement), and knowledge disparities (some team members might know more about the participants, method, topic, or audience to whom the research is directed). Talking overtly within your team about how these factors might influence research at the start of research projects can support the appropriate recognition of expertise within the group and the sharing of diverse perspectives.

RESEARCH USING INTERVIEW AND WRITTEN OR ARCHIVAL DATA

Grounded theory methods can be used to analyze a wide variety of forms of data, including written data, media, literature, posts, linguistic data, observational records, ethnographic field notes, interviews, archival data, and audio or video recordings. Often in psychology, the data collected are interview based due to their utility in developing a data set that richly answers the specific questions of a research project and represents internal processes. Researchers should select the form of data that can best provide an answer to their question, and they even may decide to use multiple forms of data in that process.

Data can be appropriate for grounded theory analyses when they have enough detail about the topic of concern. The main concern when using preexisting data sets is to establish whether the data are sufficiently rich. To decide, it can be useful to review the data with the following questions in mind: (a) If the data are not focused specifically on your question, do they provide enough information about your question to support an analysis? (b) Do the data provide a depth of information that is surprising or that can shed new light on your phenomenon? (c) Do the data provide contextual descriptions that will let you know the conditions in which certain experiences apply versus others? (If not, it will be challenging to describe when and where to apply your findings or make sense of contradictions in the data.) (d) Do the data provide enough differentiation to support a multilevel analysis of categories and subcategories? (If not, it may not make sense to conduct a grounded theory analysis and seek to develop a hierarchical system of findings.) Even though you may not know yet what the findings will be, these questions can help you identify whether a grounded theory study would be worthwhile.

MEMOING

Memoing is a practice in which all researchers on a team engage, and it serves a number of purposes, as suggested by the division of memoing into theoretical, operational, and coding memos (Glaser & Strauss, 1967; Rennie, 2000; Strauss & Corbin, 1998). There is no single correct order or time to memo. I recommend that researchers begin memoing as soon as they decide to embark on a project and that they continue, at minimum, after each interview and data analysis session.

Theoretical Memos

Centrally, memoing structures researchers' reflexive self-awareness. By that, I mean that it provides a forum to reflect on your assumptions, expectations, and hopes for your analysis. Even more, it is a space used to self-reflect so your beliefs do not have an undue influence on your analysis (e.g., by checking that your questions are not biased or actively seeking disconfirming evidence). This is the place also to reflect the ways that your experiences of personal privilege and marginalization might influence your work.

Operational Memos

Memoing also helps researchers keep track of the rationale and steps in their evolving methods. Was your protocol adjusted as you engaged in the process of theoretical sampling? If so, when and how? On what basis did you make decisions on the participants to recruit? By keeping a record of these decisions and their rationale, researchers can track them when describing their project.

Coding Memos

In addition, researchers often create coding memos, in which they consider the problem of how best to create categories and labels within their data. Writing memos supports researchers in being deliberate about the names given to findings so they represent the data well and meet their project goals. As an example, when considering how to label a category of silences described by psychotherapy clients, I began by thinking they signified "resistance" but felt it would import into my findings psychoanalytic assumptions that did not fit. I next considered calling them "withholding silences," but that seemed to imply a willfulness that did not hold across categories. I settled on calling them "disengaged silences," which I felt was reflective of the data (Levitt, 2001).

Memoing can be especially helpful within a research team because team members can refer to their memos each week to communicate the evolving changes within the analysis and share their thoughts and rationales with the team. In addition to writing memos, many grounded theory researchers use diagrams within the memoing process (see Buckley & Waring, 2013, for examples). Sketching relationships between components can support theory conceptualization. As described more in the next chapter, memoing can increase the fidelity of your findings by limiting distortions that might result from your expectations and the utility of your findings by encouraging you to consider the theoretical contributions your work will be making so that you can maximize their impact.

3 ESTABLISHING METHODOLOGICAL INTEGRITY

The concept of methodological integrity was put forward by a task force of the Society of Qualitative Inquiry in Psychology to articulate the methodological basis of trustworthiness (Lincoln & Guba, 1985)—that is, what leads us to see research as convincing. It was developed from identifying and analyzing common principles underlying prior guidelines for qualitative research (e.g., Elliott et al., 1999; Lincoln & Guba, 1985; Morrow, 2005). The purpose of a methodological integrity framework is to articulate the rationale for selecting procedures that underlie trustworthiness. In other words, it guides researchers to consider how to select and adapt procedures that best fit the purposes and characteristics of their study to strengthen the rigor of their work. Your study has *methodological integrity* when its procedures are coherent in relation to your research goals, approaches to inquiry (e.g., philosophical assumptions, epistemological approach), and study characteristics (e.g., the topic, resources, participants, researchers). As you design your study, rather than just adhering to any step-by-step guide, you are encouraged to adapt the procedures you are using to best support your specific study. See Levitt, Motulsky, et al. (2017) for a detailed description of methodological integrity within the design and review process.

https://doi.org/10.1037/0000231-003
Essentials of Critical-Constructivist Grounded Theory Research, by H. M. Levitt

In this chapter, I review in depth the two central components of methodological integrity, fidelity to the subject matter and utility of findings in meeting the study goals, in relation to grounded theory procedures and their adaptation to research goals, participants (e.g., interviewees, researchers), and other study characteristics. Throughout the book, I refer back to the concepts within methodological integrity because they can inform how you should alter the methods that you use.

FIDELITY IN CRITICAL-CONSTRUCTIVIST GROUNDED THEORY METHODS

Fidelity indicates how well your study captures the phenomenon that you are studying. Fidelity is relevant whether you conceptualize your topic as something real in the world or as a psychological construct because, in either case, your interest is to describe your topic well. For instance, although I conceptualize butch gender as a concept that is socially constructed (although with an essential basis; Levitt, 2019), I want to describe that concept and how it is socially constructed faithfully so that readers can understand that lived experience (e.g., Levitt & Hiestand, 2004). There are four concepts that researchers consider when they assess fidelity: data adequacy, perspective management during data collection, perspective management during data analysis, and groundedness.

Data Adequacy

When considering data adequacy, grounded theory researchers generally are not attempting to select participants randomly or match their participants to a population under study (see Levitt, in press, for a critical-constructivist explanation of generalization in qualitative methods). They do not seek to recruit all forms of diversity either. That strategy would not be possible because there are countless forms of diversity, and many types of diversity may not be relevant or unique in their influence on a given subject matter. Nor is there a set number of participants that is adequate across qualitative studies (although one meta-analysis suggested that 13 is the average number of participants; Levitt, Pomerville, et al., 2017).

Instead, they vary their participant selection and recruitment purposively to develop a map of the specific types of variability that will bring to light differences within the experiences and practices of their phenomenon of interest. For instance, researchers studying the experience of women's roller derby will want to consider the types of diversity that specifically influence that sport.

They might seek to interview people who play in various positions, people who have been playing varied lengths of time, and team organizers. Variations in these experiences can be expected to lead participants to construct the meaning of the sport differently. For example, newcomers might be attracted to different features than mature players. As well, during data collection and analysis, researchers will attend to variations in experience that are unexpected and recruit participants to help them better understand them. This process is similar to other deliberate sampling methods such as critical case sampling (Flyvbjerg, 2006; Patton, 2015), in which researchers seek out data that will best evaluate their developing understanding.

To meet the critical aims of their research, researchers also will want to consider how interpersonal and societal power, both internal and external to the sport, have an influence on that experience. They would consider demographic characteristics associated with variation in the experience and meaning of playing roller derby. They would want to be sure to interview players who have more power within the team (e.g., jammers and pivots). Because the sport has a punk and feminist ethic, researchers will seek out participants who can describe the meaning of these beliefs within the teams and within society (e.g., see http://youngerwomenstaskforce.blogspot.com/2006/10/roller-derby-uniting-younger-women-one.html). The consideration of power is specific to your phenomenon and the types of earned and unearned power it wields, maintains, resists, or lacks (Fine, 2016).

The scope of your question will dictate variations in the data collection process. For instance, if your research is focused on the sport nationally, you will want to consider how regional differences might influence the sport. Are there significant differences in roller derby in northern and southern states? Are there significant differences when players are in more rural or urban contexts? If you are examining roller derby within one context (e.g., examining a league), these questions will not apply. In any case, you will consider your recruitment process in relation to the types of diversity that are important within your phenomenon. If you are unsure what types are important, you can begin interviewing and ask questions that will help you learn more. This emergent process of design is supported by theoretical sampling—as you learn more about which features of your phenomenon are important, you direct your data collection accordingly. In addition, you might augment the empirical process of identifying forms of participant diversity that might be germane by reflexively examining your own lived experiences and consulting with a participant advisory group. Critical researchers often engage in power sharing or participatory designs (Teo, 2015) as they determine their research scope and agenda.

Perspective Management During Data Collection

When conducting grounded theory methods, researchers are cautious that their perspective does not unduly influence their data collection. If they inadvertently direct participants, they may not learn about their real experiences. In addition to memoing, there are a variety of ways in which researchers can seek to manage their perspectives. These can include the use of research team discussions to reflect on members' assumptions and expectations, research journals, and bracketing—that is, the process in which researchers become aware of their assumptions about and perspectives on their phenomenon so that they can endeavor to place them to the side to prevent them from unduly influencing their research (Giorgi, 2009). From a constructivist approach to grounded theory, there is not the assumption that you can completely set aside your perspective. After all, many assumptions are outside of your awareness, and you may not recognize their influence. Also, your language structures your experience, and there is no neutral language. The idea of *fallible memoing* (Rennie, 2000) can be a useful construct to guide grounded theory research. This idea holds that as a researcher, even though you realize that you cannot excise all influence on your subject matter, you should attempt to avoid undue influence when possible. Also, it means working to recognize and transparently report influences that you think were present in your data collection.

The desire to limit your influence on respondents' answers during data collection does not mean that you cannot decide on the questions that you would like to ask participants. If your work is theory driven (e.g., psychoanalytic theory, feminist theory), these interests will structure the questions you ask and the sources you use. But you do not want to lead participants or select sources to confirm your beliefs. Your analysis will be stronger if it considers a diversity of responses. As you structure your research, it can be helpful for you to reflect on the perspective management practices that would work best for you. These can entail both learning about your own positions (e.g., those that are more dominant or marginalized) and how they influence your experiences of your topic, as well as deciding on procedures to assist you to continue this reflexive self-examination. There are a variety of procedures that you may choose to bring to bear to check on your data collection. For instance, you might decide to use a member check and ask participants to review their own interviews to see whether they are clear and comprehensive. You might use a participatory method and consult with community members, users, or stakeholders in your research project to see whether they would suggest questions or areas of inquiry for your analysis. These sorts of checks are not necessary but might facilitate your research goals, depending on your topic.

Perspective Management During Data Analysis

Researchers are not only concerned with managing their perspectives during data collection but also through the process of analysis as well. Critical and constructivist researchers tend to manage their perspectives in two ways (Levitt, Motulsky, et al., 2017). You may consider whether you will be using one or both of these approaches as you design and report your study. The first way is that they will attempt to limit the influence of their perspective, using the same procedures described already (e.g., memoing).

The second route is more common for grounded theory research driven by critical approaches to research (or other theory-driven research). In these approaches, you are using your theory as a lens to guide your analysis (e.g., multicultural theory, critical queer theory). The main distinction in using this lens is that you will need to be transparent, not only about your research questions but also that this perspective was used in structuring your inquiry so that readers understand the process by which you analyzed your data. These studies are not intended to evaluate the theory but to identify the experiences or processes that applying the theory reveals. For instance, if you are studying the experience of being a female engineering professor from a feminist lens, you are not evaluating feminism per se, but are using that perspective to help identify what that work experience entails. The theory is a tool to increase your perspicacity.

Like managing your perspective in the data collection process, you might use procedures such as member checking or getting feedback from community members or members of a participatory research team to give you feedback on a summary of your findings. Ultimately, however, because you are the researcher and have access to the perspectives of all the participants in your study (while people providing feedback may not), you will need to decide how best to reconcile any feedback with your other data. More detail on this process is presented in Chapter 5.

Groundedness

Grounded theory studies typically use quotations from data sources or interviews to illustrate the nature of their analyses. Typically, for every main finding (or *cluster*), I will provide at least a few quotes to illustrate the meaning therein. (If possible, I will strive to have a quote for every category therein.) This practice brings to life the experiences of the participants and deepens readers' understanding of the phenomenon while permitting an evaluation of the analytic process. Because grounded theory results sections usually present discrete ideas across multiple categories and clusters, they may require even more quotes than other qualitative methods. This process tends to add to the length of manuscripts, however, so it can be good to consider this in relation to the journal selected.

There are two ways in which you can manage these demands if pages limits are severe. One is by having your results section focus on the cluster level of the hierarchy (immediately under your core category). This can allow you a couple of quotes illustrating each cluster instead of one for each category. Another strategy that can be useful when the page limits are stringent (as in medical journals, which might have 5,000-word limits) is to remove the quotes from the main manuscript and place them in supplemental material (L. Granek, personal communication, June 11, 2019). This practice can allow readers and reviewers to access the quotes online and allow the paper to be printed within the journal guidelines.

UTILITY IN GROUNDED THEORY METHODS

Because grounded theory methods are applied for a range of reasons, you should not assume that your reader knows the goals for your study. Grounded theory methods initially were proposed as a way to develop a theory to explain a phenomenon, form hypotheses, and create sociological and ethnographic accounts, and most often in psychology, they are used to develop a description of a psychological experience. These methods also can be implemented within a critical framework in which there are goals to create social change, raise consciousness of implicit workings of power, or generate alternatives to oppression. Being clear on the purpose of your study will allow researchers to understand whether or not you have met your goal. Four elements of utility can be useful to consider in this process: contextualization, catalyst for insight, meaningful contributions, and coherence between findings.

Contextualization

When reporting your research, providing information on the characteristics of your participants will allow readers to better transfer the findings to their own contexts. You can do this by describing the place, time, and social and ideological context of your research in your introduction. In the methods section, you can provide information on your participants that indicates their specific context. Through the results section, you can provide context to aid the reader in interpreting quotes. For instance, "My students are struggling to pay attention in the classroom" will be understood differently if it is a quote from a teacher of students with attentional disorders or a teacher of students in a school system that has just canceled their lunch program. Prefacing quotes with key contextual factors makes them intelligible. And through the discussion section, researchers will consider the implications of their research as they relate to varied contexts and note where future research is needed.

Qualitative research is often valued for its ability to provide detailed, in-depth local knowledge that can be useful in understanding causal processes, meanings and their consequences, and the relationship between context and cause (Maxwell, 2012). For instance, if you are studying power relationships within mentoring, the cultural backgrounds of the mentor and mentee will be important contextual factors to examine because there are varied cultural norms on mentoring. Report those factors that will influence the interpretation of your findings.

Catalyst for Insight

To produce findings that will have utility, you will have to collect data that contain the potential for innovative insights. To enhance the potential that this will occur, you might consider how to help participants feel comfortable with disclosure in interviews. Thinking about differences in privilege that might exist between you and your participants (e.g., race, class, or educational privilege) can allow you to better minimize differences that might make your interviewee feel unsafe sharing their experiences with you. For instance, if you are a heterosexual person interviewing bisexual people, it can be helpful to make clear that you are working with an affirmative research team to learn about their experiences of stigma and to be sensitive to their concerns. The ways to best create safety will depend on the specific features of your issue and participants.

Both constructivist and critical researchers see it as beneficial when investigators have a depth of experience with the phenomenon they are studying. For instance, the effects of playing roller derby will be more meaningful to you if you are a member of a team. The implicit communications within the dynamics of a community will become evident if you live in that community for long enough because you can bring ethnographic insights that you have gained through interactions and observations. Your experiences would not replace the analysis of the data provided by your sources (Rennie, 1998), but they provide a sensitivity that allows you to notice implicit meanings that you might have missed otherwise. Similarly, recruiting participants who have a depth of experience will benefit your project.

Meaningful Contributions

In the framework that methodological integrity provides, the judgment of whether you have succeeded will depend largely on what your goals were (e.g., deepening understanding, advancing social justice goals, developing hypotheses). Results can be useful for many reasons, and all studies do not need to produce entirely new findings. Confirming a finding that was questioned or extending it to a new context can have utility.

With regard to the process of developing innovative results, though, there has been a longstanding debate in the grounded theory community about whether researchers should familiarize themselves with the literature on their topic before their research begins. The concern is that this reading might act to constrain the researcher's ability to organize the data in a novel manner (Glaser, 1998; Glaser & Strauss, 1967). There have been differences in opinion on this point, however (Charmaz, 2014; Strauss & Corbin, 1990), and it seems that opinion has swayed so that it is more typical now that grounded theory researchers become familiar with the literature surrounding their topics because it can also sensitize them to aspects of an experience and pressing related issues. I recommend this too. At the same time, researchers can use methods, such as bracketing and memoing, to become aware of how their expectations might influence the creation of their findings and to limit those effects.

Coherence Between Findings

When you conduct your interviews, you may notice that there are times at which participants have conflicting opinions. It can help to notice these tensions while interviewing because it can guide you to ask questions about the basis of conflicts. Your goal is not to emphasize commonalities in a manner that masks differences (Bettez, 2015; Clarke, 2009), but to present patterns and divergences in a way that enhances their utility.

You will want to explain the reasons for conflict so that readers know how to use your findings. If one finding says that a work climate is good, and another says it is not good, consumers will not know how to apply the finding. Specifying when, why, and for whom a finding holds is necessary. Sometimes you can find in data sources rationales for experiences and beliefs. For instance, there may be experiences rooted in their development that participants can recount. At other times, though, you may need to adopt a historical or sociological perspective to see these patterns. For example, it may be that in an institution under study, one generation of women resists sexism by forming their own social groups and gaining interpersonal support that way, and another generation resists sexism by labeling it and seeking full integration. These differences might not make sense at first but might make more sense when considering the supports the generations could access, both within the institution and society at large. In any case, describing context and motivations and reasons for differences will bolster the utility of your findings by guiding readers on how to apply them.

Future chapters describe the procedures typically used in critical-constructivist grounded theory; the successful application of these methods will depend on the adaptation of the methods to your specific project. Discussing the methodological integrity of your work can be useful in the initial writing of your manuscript, especially when you have adapted procedures so they are more attuned to your question, topic, or participants. As well, describing how your work has methodological integrity is especially important when responding to reviews of your work (see Levitt, Motulsky, et al., 2017, for principles of methodological integrity created to respond to common misunderstandings that occur in reviews of qualitative research). This concept can support you in justifying the adaptations you have made to your procedures to develop findings that are more fitting for your research project.

4

COLLECTING THE DATA

The process of collecting data is at least as important as the analysis. If the data that you collect are not interesting and do not contain descriptions that will lead to new ideas and conceptualizations, the results of the analysis will not be innovative. As a grounded theory researcher, you can take a number of steps to make it more likely that your data will permit you to produce a meaningful contribution and address the research problems you are considering. In this chapter, the processes of selecting, recruiting, and interviewing participants and how to maintain the researcher–participant alliance are discussed. Because grounded theory research in psychology often is interview based, this will be the focus of the chapter, but similar principles can be applied when using grounded theory with survey-based, written, or archival data.

SELECTING AND RECRUITING PARTICIPANTS

When considering how to recruit and select participants and data sources, there are two central and interconnected factors to consider. The first is the role of *data adequacy* within methodological integrity (see Chapter 3, this

https://doi.org/10.1037/0000231-004
Essentials of Critical-Constructivist Grounded Theory Research, by H. M. Levitt

volume; Levitt, Motulsky, et al., 2017), which holds across qualitative methods. In the process of seeking adequate data for analysis, the researchers consider the diversity of perspectives and types of engagement that are being conveyed by participants. They seek enough diversity to help them develop a thorough understanding of their subject matter. For instance, in a study on loss, if only people who have lost partners through illness are interviewed, data would not support the application of findings to other types of loss.

Some factors influence a broad range of human experiences, such as race, ethnicity, and gender, and so diversity within them typically is important to seek, but there may be many other such factors, depending on your question and research goals. From a critical perspective, considering how privilege, oppression, and systemic differences influence the experiences you are studying can help you decide the types of participants to recruit to understand the workings of your phenomenon fully.

For instance, if you are conducting a study on the communication about loss of a life partner, including participants who are not in married heterosexual relationships (e.g., who have been common-law partners or in a gay relationship) will be important because their relationships may not be valued in the same way, and their loss might be perceived differently. If you are conducting a study on schoolteachers in California, recruiting teachers from school systems in areas with varied socioeconomic contexts will be important. As a researcher, you set the scope of your question. You might decide to study only teachers in San Francisco, in which case teachers from Los Angeles would not be recruited, but then you would consider regional differences within the city that might produce distinctive teaching experiences. This process will allow you to improve the fidelity in your research by permitting you to describe central distinctions within the experience of your phenomenon.

The second related process, which originated in grounded theory methods, is *theoretical sampling* (Glaser & Strauss, 1967). In this process, researchers collect data and engage in analysis in waves, examining their evolving analysis to see where there are gaps in understanding. This process allows you to consider the types of participants needed to help you develop a comprehensive conceptualization of your topic. For instance, in conducting an analysis of an early wave of data collection in a study on female executives, researchers may notice that the experience of a woman with children is strikingly different from those who were not mothers. This observation may lead researchers to deliberately recruit more mothers in the next wave so their experiences can be integrated into the ongoing analysis. As your conceptualization evolves, you will look for aspects that are less well understood to guide your selection and recruitment of participants across your study and strengthen its fidelity because they provide a clearer picture of the phenomenon as it is experienced with its variations.

DEVELOPING AN INTERVIEW PROTOCOL AND INTERVIEWING

Grounded theory researchers in psychology typically use semistructured interviews (Levitt, Pomerville, et al., 2017), although any interviewing style can be adopted when using these methods. In developing questions, I ask myself what questions will help me to (a) develop a clear and in-depth understanding of the topic, (b) best meet the goals of my research project, and (c) respect the experiences of the participants and understand their contexts.

Your epistemological perspective and goals guide the questions that you ask. For instance, if the project aims to sensitize clinicians to a dynamic in therapy sessions, make policy recommendations to an organization, or to develop an intervention, your questions will seek the kind of knowledge that will be best suited to the nature of those goals (e.g., How might a clinical theory, policy, or intervention be more helpful?). This section describes these considerations.

Considering Positionality in the Interview Context

The principle of perspective management during the data collection process guides researchers to develop self-awareness and become reflexive (Burman, 2006; Morawski, 2005) so that they can recognize the hazards that their expectations and perspectives may pose to data collection. Privileges attributed to people with dominant or majority statuses (e.g., being White, cisgender, heterosexual, able-bodied, a citizen of the country in which you live) can be difficult to recognize because they are normalized in our society. (It is challenging to be aware of all of the routine benefits I have from being White because it is impossible to notice each time that I do not face discrimination.) Developing an awareness of what you do not experience takes work. If your questions only focus on the privileged side of an experience, the understanding you develop will be necessarily narrowed. This idea is the central thesis of feminist standpoint perspectives that argue that what you can see is influenced by your position—seeking views from the margins is essential for comprehensive understanding (Harding, 2015). For instance, in a study about literacy, I might not think to ask questions about access to books during childhood because there were many books in my family's home. Because people have many identities, it can be important to consider the systems of stressors that generate both your areas of privilege and marginalization to determine how they might affect your interview process (see Moradi & Grzanka, 2017).

It will also benefit you to be open to new learning about power in relation to both your participants and yourself through the course of your study. For instance, in a study on HIV for young gay, bisexual, transgender, or queer men of color, I might not recognize the influence of house and gay family systems on my participants because they are outside my cultural experience, and I might brush these relationships to the side as tangential rather than exploring their effects. I might need to change my interview protocol to examine the effects of this system and challenge my ideas of family, resilience, and the functions of minority stressors.

Critical researchers often begin their work with both a desire to challenge experiences of oppression and marginalization as well as some unconscious internalization of the dominant beliefs of their society (Levitt, Morrill, et al., in press). Ironically, each of these sets of beliefs can make it difficult to recognize the other. And they can coexist within researchers who have either marginalized or privileged identities. As a result, it can be crucial for investigators to engage in processes such as memoing, research team reflection, and learning more about their phenomenon to consider the limits of their own experiences and their assumptions. These forms of structured reflexivity can guide you to seek knowledge that you might be missing about the communities and topics that you are studying so you can use appropriate recruitment methods, shape attuned questions, and obtain insightful data. Adopting a humble attitude of self-examination and learning from the lived experiences of your participants can help you avoid microaggressions (e.g., see Shelton & Delgado-Romero, 2013) that occur when researchers inadvertently communicate to their participants prejudicial assumptions from stigmatizing or colonialist belief systems (Tuhiwai Smith, 2012).

Researchers who share an identity with participants may have the advantages of bringing to the research a deeper understanding of the phenomenon under study and what is needed, but they may have to contend with issues due to both that similarity, such as confidentiality concerns due to being in the same community, or assumptions of oversimilarity. Also, the impact of their divergent experiences, potentially educational and socioeconomic differences, may take them by surprise. For instance, it may take a good deal of reflection for researchers to consider how their varied intersections of stressors and privileges (e.g., academic culture) shape their questions, investments, and assumptions (e.g., Zavella, 1993). Conducting this self-reflection as much as possible in advance of your interviews can allow you to be more open to hearing the experiences of your participants.

Researchers also can take care to study principles of culturally sensitive interviewing skills (e.g., Arczynski et al., 2018). Critical researchers consider how their presence might inadvertently influence data collection. For instance, their visible identities (e.g., gender, race) and their status as a researcher and/or clinician may communicate significant power differentials that influence what participants feel comfortable disclosing or that elicit or discourage participation (Ellis et al., 2007). Acknowledging and addressing differences in power, sensitively phrasing questions (Bemak & Chung, 2017), stating shared values, and communicating advocacy goals for the research project (Castillo et al., 2007) may make your participants feel comfortable discussing their experiences.

In addition, critical researchers consider the political context of their participants and the possible risks they face by participating. You might realize that many participants (e.g., domestic violence survivors, undocumented immigrants) may not feel safe enough to participate in research. Or participants might not understand the differences between you as a researcher from a university and a government agent with whom that they are required to speak. It will be imperative that you are able to communicate your research purpose and adjust your research goals so you can provide a safe context.

How and What to Ask?

When developing an interview protocol for grounded theory studies, it is helpful to begin by letting the participants know that you see them as the experts on their own experience and that you are hoping to learn from them. It can be daunting to be interviewed, and participants may feel cowed by talking with someone with academic degrees, so being clear about your role as learner can be an empowering reposition. I usually begin interviews by telling the interviewee my central question (e.g., "What is your experience of being someone who is X or has done X?"), and I ask them to let me know in the interview anything relevant to that question. Sometimes participants have ideas to share immediately, and sometimes they require prompts to stimulate their thinking. To avoid undue influence of participants, interview subquestions are usually organized by questions about your topic, questions to check conceptualizations, and credibility questions.

Questions About Your Topic

It will help to shape your questions to meet your research goals. Because I tend to explore ideas from a critical-constructivist perspective, I am interested in exploring how meanings are constructed. I often ask how participants learned about a topic, how their expectations about an experience differed from their actual experience, how they communicate about an experience to sets of significant others, or how they made sense of an experience as it unfolded.

To create a safe space for discussing issues that might be sensitive to discuss or culturally taboo, I sometimes share my own identities and express my affirmative stance or interest in developing supports for a community or an issue. To explore the influence of their social and systemic context, you might ask how the topic transpires in varied social contexts (e.g., childhood, workplace, relationships). You can ask whether they have any cultural experiences or identities (privileged or marginalized) that might influence that experience. I often will list examples that might be relevant to the topic (e.g., religious, racial, gender, sexual orientation, immigration status). You might ask how institutions shape the experience of a topic or how the media portrays it and whether this affects their experience. Or you could ask when and how they feel supported or feel a lack of support in relation to an experience. Often, I will review the literature and consult with people who have had that experience (as coresearchers or advisors) to guide the development of my questions so that they can focus on issues that are of concern to the community at hand.

If your goal is to develop a theoretical framework from your analysis, it can be particularly helpful to consider including more abstract questions that can undergird that development. In the process of theory development, Strauss and Corbin (1998) recommended that you consider the internal and external (or structural) causal and intervening *conditions* for your phenomenon, the *actions and interactional strategies* in use, and the *consequences* associated with your phenomenon; you may use these ideas to guide your questions and illuminate these relationships. Others (Charmaz, 2014; Glaser, 1992; Rennie, 1998) have seen that process as overly structured and potentially interfering with the emergence of a theory.

I recommend that you consider the relationships and definitions that seem most important for you to understand and shape questions about them. Typically, I find that simply asking questions about how my phenomenon is experienced and how it functions across relevant contexts is sufficient to obtain answers to many of these higher order questions. In any case, you may wish to consider whether the questions you are asking will provide answers to conceptualization at the level and form that is appropriate to your aims (for more on the development of theory in the analytic process, see Chapter 5). This can be important to think through because you do not have the data to ground the analyses that are important to you, and it will be hard for you to have confidence in your conclusions later on.

In general, questions should be organized from the most general to the more specific. That order prevents the more specific questions from narrowing the possible answers given to broader questions. For instance, if I asked my participants about how having access to electronic library databases influenced their curiosity before asking how they meet curiosity, it might cause the participants to focus on the library searches and ignore other aspects. Taking care to word questions in a way that does not communicate assumptions will assist in this process.

Questions to Check Conceptualizations

Sometimes, you might ask a question or two to evaluate an evolving conceptualization—perhaps developed from an initial wave of analysis. In this case, you still want to be as open as possible in your question while you seek the participants' reactions to an idea. For instance, you might say, "It sounds like you are saying that you became more curious when you felt a newfound support for your intellectualism—does this fit for you or would something else perhaps fit better?" I take care to give participants an option to disagree with or adjust any idea that I advance and place those remarks at the end of the interview to give participants time to consolidate their thinking and not to be swayed.

Credibility Questions

At the end of the interview, I always include credibility questions, both to assess the comprehensiveness of my interview and to provide the participants with a chance to add missing data. In addition to asking for general feedback on the interview, these questions typically include "Is there anything that I haven't asked that you feel would help me understand the central concern of the interview?" and "Is there anything about me [my position, race, gender, your knowing or not knowing me] that might have made it difficult to share something about your experience?" In both cases, if the participant replies "yes," I can ask them to elaborate, and then that missing data can be included in the interview.

Interviewing Skills

Strong data collection often rests on the development of interviewing skills, including the development of attuned listening and facilitative skills (Josselson, 2013). Learning about interviewing strategies and practicing interviewing is crucial. When I teach classes and workshops on qualitative research, I usually emphasize the following three skills that I see as central to interviewing but challenging to integrate: using nonleading, open-minded questions; staying on topic; and developing depth.

Using Nonleading, Open-Minded Questions

A common concern when developing interview questions is that participants might adopt perspectives to please you; defer to your ideas, think you have more expertise; or close down and stop communicating their own experiences. Developing a nonleading interview protocol and developing interview skills will help you in this regard. All the questions should be delivered in a manner that is as nonleading as possible so as not to inadvertently communicate your assumptions, expectations, and beliefs about what participants' answers should be. For instance, instead of asking, "How has your experience of being a graduate student influenced your sense of curiosity?" you might first want to ask, "Has your experience of being a graduate student influenced your sense of curiosity? If so, how?" This latter phrasing does not assume that there was any influence. Subtleties like this should be carefully examined to ensure that you are not making undue assumptions within your protocol.

Having an open-minded attitude can be especially important when interviewing participants who relay beliefs that you find objectional, such as people who hold or misuse their positions of privilege. For instance, when interviewing faith leaders who argued that women experiencing domestic violence could not obtain a divorce because they believed that marriage was sanctified by God or that women's duty was to be submissive to their husbands' will (e.g., Levitt & Ware, 2006), showing the emotions I felt would have made them shut down. Instead, responding with curiosity prompted them to elaborate more about the underlying thinking that supported this mode of thinking and allowed for a stronger analysis of the systemic issues at play. It allowed me to convey why they held beliefs that were mystifying to me before and suggest how to address those beliefs. Prejudicial or offensive attitudes can arise in any interview, however, so it is helpful to consider how you would like to respond beforehand and what supports you might need to examine the premises for offensive ideas. It can allow you to shed light on these ideas in your research while still taking care of yourself.

Staying on Topic

It can be challenging at times to keep verbose interviewees focused on the research question. Questions such as "How does that relate to [the interview topic]?" can be helpful. Researchers may need to find ways to interrupt their participants in a manner that feels comfortable to them, given their interpersonal and cultural backgrounds. I encourage researchers to consider these strategies before the interview. They can include statements such as "That idea is really interesting, and I'd like to hear more about it after the interview, but let's return to the interview focus for now."

Staying on topic can be especially tricky when your topic is one that examines the relationship between multiple phenomena. For instance, in a study on how housing instability influences youths' school experience, asking participants about their experience of housing instability and then asking about their experience of being in school can keep you from answering the central question of the study: how these questions intersect. While you can ask some of these questions, most of your interview should focus on the intersection of these experiences: How does one influence the other? Although you might bring a critical perspective to bear on the stories they tell and might identify types of systemic interactions that they do not recognize, asking them directly about their experience of the mutual influences in your question will give you information that will contribute to your conceptualization of this interaction.

Developing Depth

To develop an interview that has the level of detail needed for a grounded theory interview, researchers will want to continue exploring answers to questions until they have obtained a *thick description* of their experiences (Geertz, 1973), a detailed description that brings to life an experience and how it shifts across contexts. Instead of moving quickly from one question to the next, this process requires that you consider whether you fully understand the answers given and continue to explore it. For instance, when asked about the experience of curiosity in graduate school, a participant might reply, "I felt that I was suddenly expected to ask questions. It was demanded of me in my assignments and classes." Instead of moving to the next questions, you can flesh out that experience by pausing to allow more time or by saying, for example, "Tell me more," "What was it like to have this expectation?" or "How was this expectation communicated?" An in-depth understanding can reveal contextual, relational, emotional, and systemic information that can guide the analysis.

It will be especially important to clarify the meanings associated with slang, metaphors, and emotional terms because they can mean very different things to different people. For instance, "feeling frustrated" might indicate anger to one participant, sadness to another, and fear to a third. You will be glad to have information on all these levels when you begin to conduct your analysis and wonder how to understand the meanings conveyed.

Practicing these three sets of skills in one or two mock interviews can be helpful because it can take a while to learn to combine them effectively. Record your interview, and then review it. Ask yourself if you were nonleading and on topic and whether you were able to achieve a deep and contextualized understanding of the experience of your participant.

RESEARCHER–PARTICIPANT ALLIANCE: WHO SHOULD ASK WHAT AND HOW TO ESTABLISH RAPPORT

During the interview process, researchers will wish to help participants feel comfortable disclosing information. Being transparent about your research will allow participants to develop trust in you. Using empathic responses and reflections can help the participant to feel heard and accepted. Because they typically have greater experiential expertise than you do (Foss & Foss, 2011), you will want to be careful that you are not adding information to the interview that might lead the participants to veer away from their conceptualization and pressure them to adopt your own (e.g., asking participants whether they endorse your theory vs. asking them what they experience or understand).

When considering qualitative research from a critical-constructivist perspective, it can be helpful to consider both how to present oneself and how to help the participant feel most comfortable sharing their experience and ask perceptive yet sensitive questions. For instance, should I come to an interview in a suit and introduce myself as Dr. Levitt, university professor, or should I wear jeans and go by Heidi? Maybe a different interviewer would be better. Should an interviewer share the same identities as the participants (e.g., gender, race) or not? In addition to considering interviewing skills, I consider several factors in interviewing: knowledge about a subject and power imbalance and trust.

Knowledge About a Subject

On one hand, if you know more about a subject, you may be able to ask more penetrating questions during the interview. This can be advantageous, especially if the participant may be withholding or less able to articulate their experiences without support. On the other hand, sometimes, if you are seen as knowing too much, participants may not elaborate on their experience because they think you already understand what they mean. For this reason, we decided it was advantageous to have a graduate student interview our expert therapist participants because it might encourage additional explanation (Levitt & Williams, 2010). When I share the same identity as my participants (e.g., lesbian, gay, bisexual, transgender, and queer [LGBTQ] research), I tell participants that even though I may understand a situation, I will ask questions to hear their experience in their own words. This practice makes me feel more comfortable asking questions to which a community member should know the answer.

Power Imbalance and Trust

Like knowledge, the appearance of power and concerns about how it is wielded can either benefit or restrict disclosure in an interview, and it can be helpful to consider how it might influence your interview. For instance, when interviewing clergy in the U.S. South on the interaction of faith and domestic violence, I behaved quite formally to respect their social norms. Even though the religious leaders had more power than I did within the city, I was aware that the leaders might worry about how I, as the researcher, might present what they communicated to me. In that context, my professional credentials were evidence that I would seek to present the findings scientifically and not sensationally.

When interviewing young men in our LGBTQ community center on sexual safety, I tried to gain trust by being more casual and sensitive to the social norms in that context. When interviewing the religious leaders, I did not share my lesbian identity, while at the community center, I did in every interview because it was relevant to building a connection and assuaging concerns that I might use the data in a heterosexist manner. As a researcher, it can help to consider the types of privilege and marginalization that you carry and how it might influence your connection with interviewees. Learning about the social systems that you will be entering can allow you to present yourself appropriately, alert you to the concerns of your participants, and demonstrate conscientiousness and respect.

RESEARCH ETHICS

It is helpful to be familiar with the ethics code of your profession to guide you in your research process (e.g., American Psychological Association [APA], 2017). Also, in advance of contact with any participants, you may want to check your institution's research review board to see whether you require approval for projects you are conducting. In this section, I review some common ethical concerns for you to consider as you plan your study.

Do No Harm

It is incumbent on you as a qualitative researcher to consider the demands you are placing on your participants and whether they are justified (APA, 2017).

Consider whether the gains for the participants are worth the demands of participating in the research. For instance, if you are studying people who have had a traumatic experience, consider the supports you might need to have in place for them to feel comfortable disclosing. Is interviewing them face-to-face at your university meeting your needs while making it more challenging for interviewees to feel safe? Is it necessary to ask them to revisit the trauma once again by asking them to provide feedback on your findings, especially if it reaches them when they are unprepared to reencounter these memories? There are many ways to establish the credibility of your work, the central one being the analytic process itself. Generally, it is important to consider how to reduce the burden that research places, especially on vulnerable participants.

It can be important for you to remember that, historically, research has had adverse impacts on many marginalized groups. Researchers can expect legitimate resistance to research that should be respected and may require developing longer term relationships and adopting a critical framework that views participants as collaborators and codirectors of research (Tuck & Yang, 2014). For instance, after a history of having researchers come into their communities, try an intervention, and then leave precipitously, American Indian communities have developed sets of regulations for researchers to protect themselves from problem-focused approaches and to support these communities in shaping their own futures (see https://www.ncai.org/policy-research-center/research-data/prc-publications). As a researcher, you may want to consider what you can give back to the participants. Can you present your findings in a way that will assist them or their community? Can you publish your research to shed light on the issues with which they have entrusted you? Can you use your research in advocacy for policy or institutional changes that could benefit them? Although research participation always has some cost to participants, you will want to ensure it is not too taxing and consider how your research can advantage those who are supporting your work.

The Consent Process

Researchers want to be sure that participants understand the nature of the study, how the data they share will be used, risks and benefits of participating, and that they are participating voluntarily (APA, 2017). Researchers should keep in mind that consent in qualitative research is typically considered to be processual. This means that participants can give or withhold their consent at any point in the research because consent is seen as a process. Because participants might be discussing questions that are sensitive or painful to discuss, it might be that they are comfortable with one question but not the next. It is okay if a participant cries or feels emotional during an interview, so long as they are okay doing so. You should convey to your participants that they can let you know if they would not like to answer any question. If they need a break, to get a glass of water, or to recommence the interview on another day, you should be prepared to support that decision. Also, because questions may evolve in an interview process, you will want to indicate to your institutional review board when you are engaging in unstructured or semistructured interviews so that you feel comfortable exploring unexpected issues as they arise.

Confidentiality and Data Sharing

In your consent process, you will want to be clear with your participants who will have access to their data. If you are not sure who exactly will have access to the data, you should identify the people in general terms (e.g., "three undergraduate research assistants in psychology at my university"). You also may alert your research team to confidentiality issues and let them know that if they suspect they might be able to identify a participant, they should let you know immediately. It can help to remind your research team that you are a representative of your profession and so should always model respect for your participants. For instance, you should not talk about your data, even in general terms, in a public space because it might cause any listeners to question your ethics and feel suspect about the research.

Maintaining confidentiality can be more complicated for qualitative researchers because quoted material is often required that provides contextual information that can be revealing. Also, critical research projects often focus on people who have marginalized identities, and the intersection of their demographic characteristics may inadvertently disclose their identities (e.g., how many Jewish lesbian qualitative psychologists are there in Boston?). Researchers have to take care that their participants' identities are well concealed if they are promising confidentiality, which may mean aggregating the demographic information or masking it.

More recently, researchers are being asked to engage in data sharing, which means that researchers agree to give their raw data to other professionals either to assess the rigor of their work (as in the case of journal editors) or to confirm their findings independently (as in the case of other research teams). This process is not uncommon with large quantitative data sets for which confidentiality of data can more easily be guaranteed. The reasons for sharing data are to ascertain the rigor of analyses and their replicability.

In its *Publication Manual*, APA (2020) has discouraged data sharing for qualitative researchers, however, and advised caution in this process for a number of reasons: (a) It may not be possible to guarantee confidentiality with data sets that provide the level of contextual detail that is common in qualitative analyses—a concern that is particularly pertinent for people who have marginalized identities and may be easier to identify; (b) the time-intensive process of masking data may remove contextual information needed for its analysis and render it meaningless; (c) quoted material is typically provided within a qualitative manuscript that reviewers can use to evaluate the groundedness of an analysis; (d) participants may be willing to partici-pate in research by a particular set of researchers because they trust them to analyze their data (e.g., an LGBTQ+ affirmative research team) and that consent may not extend to other researchers (e.g., a team that is not affirma-tive); and (e) qualitative researchers tend not to expect findings to replicate across researchers who do not share the same theoretical frameworks (e.g., critical theories) and research goals (Tuval-Mashiach, 2020), undermining the purpose of sharing findings. Despite these concerns, if you decide to share the raw data you collect with reviewers or other research teams, you should make this clear in your consent form before you collect data.

Boundary Issues

It will be important that you keep in mind your role as interviewer and do not slip into a therapist role because participants have not consented to engage in therapy. You want to keep the interview focused on the topic that they have agreed to discuss, but it might be helpful to provide or have on hand mental health or other referrals (e.g., advocacy organizations, shelter information, support groups) if they might be relevant to your study topic.

Also, when conducting research within your own community, you may want to consider the ethics of having members disclose personal information to you. Will their disclosure act to harm them or reduce their sense of security in their social network? When I conducted interviews in a lesbian community that I was part of, it seemed to me that it would create a power imbalance if I were to see participants in the community after I had intimate informa-tion about them, and they knew little about me. As a result, I gave them the opportunity after the interview to ask me questions if they were interested. My feminist ethics guided me toward this decision (Levitt & Hiestand, 2004), although I also felt safe enough in that context to invite personal questions and might not have done so in another context (e.g., in a context that was not LGBTQ-affirmative). When making your own decisions on how to maintain an alliance with your participants, issues related to safety and ethics should be considered together.

5 ANALYZING THE DATA AND PRODUCING RESULTS

In this chapter, I describe the central steps of grounded theory, providing tips and examples, and the process through which it develops findings. Then, I discuss specific checks on methodological integrity that you can integrate. Finally, I consider how a critical-constructivist lens can influence and enrich your engagement with these processes.

CREATING MEANING UNITS AND LABELING THEM

The process of *unitizing* is one in which researchers divide their text into manageable chunks for analysis. Units can be created within interviews or other forms of data. In the approach that was developed by Rennie (2000), the process of creating units was drawn from descriptive phenomenological methods (Giorgi, 2009). *Meaning units* are initial responses, drawn from the original interviews or texts, that each provides a preliminary answer to the question of your study. This process combines the *conceptualization* and *open coding* processes described in Strauss and Corbin's (1998) versions of grounded theory (I note this for readers familiar with that approach). In their

https://doi.org/10.1037/0000231-005
Essentials of Critical-Constructivist Grounded Theory Research, by H. M. Levitt

process, researchers use a coding paradigm to make notes (typically line by line or by sentence or paragraph), labeling and naming various processes, conditions, and events before engaging in unitizing data (e.g., Strauss & Corbin, 1998). (Others who view the use of a coding paradigm as either optional or as problematic include Charmaz, 2014; Glaser, 1992; and Rennie, 2000.)

In the unitizing process that I use, text is conceptualized into units that each contain one central meaning related to the question under study (so units might extend across lines of text), and then its content is conceptualized and labeled simultaneously. I find this approach to be much more efficient because (a) it considerably reduces the time it takes to engage in this initial step, (b) it orients me to think about meanings in my data as they relate to my study aims right from the start, (c) it keeps me (and my students) from getting bogged down in naming processes that are not relevant to my question or study purpose and becoming overwhelmed, and (d) it allows my understanding to emerge without a preconceived structure. In fact, I encourage my students to place a sticky note with their research question on the side of their computer screen, so they remember to create units and unit labels that answer that question. The following are some tips on how to create units effectively.

Creating Meaning Units

Typically, all the information in a text or transcript will not be relevant to the question you are asking. Text that does not seem relevant can be omitted or included in a following or prior unit to provide context for the text that addresses your study question. For instance, if the researchers ask an interviewee about her experience of learning to conduct therapy, the response might be:

> I remember having a moment where I was really scared during my first practi-cum. I was at home and ready to leave to catch the bus to the counseling center. I was already worried about being late because the bus was not so regular. And I thought, "What if I don't know how to help someone, and they become worse, and it's my fault?" I thought about my sister, though, and that kept me going. She had this terrible relationship, and her husband was insulting her all the time and cutting her off from her friends. Her husband had a job working in a software company, and he was working late all the time on this project to create voice-activated responses, but when he did see her, he was horrible. She wanted to leave the relationship, but she felt so alone. She told me afterwards that what I did that helped her the most was show that I cared about her and wanted her to be okay. It gave her the courage to keep caring about herself and to find a way out. So, I might not need to have all the answers, but I know how to support someone to find their own way.

As you can see, there are many discrete meanings in this unit of text. Some of the text is not relevant at all to the topic of learning to conduct therapy, like the description of the potentially late bus and her sister's husband working at a software company and his project. But, overall, the participant is sharing one idea in answer to the question about learning to become a therapist. Whenever she turns to a new idea, a new meaning unit would be formed. For instance, if she continued by saying, "I also learned how to notice what my own emotions were telling me about my clients. I realized how my clients like to make people feel and what this tells me about their sense of their own position interpersonally," it would signal a new answer to the study question and so necessitates a new unit.

Creating Meaning Unit Labels

As you divide the text into units, you will label their meaning. Rather than labeling units with one word or a short phrase, I recommend assigning a label to each unit that is specific and makes clear the way the unit answers your study question—typically structured as a sentence or sentence fragment (e.g., "She projected her need for intimacy onto her therapist and then felt he was seeking to be intrusive"; "Lesbian aunt being shunned by my family and by me was my first encounter with heterosexism"). Especially in a critical-constructivist analysis, the clearer you are about the varied meanings, functions, and contexts related to your study question, the easier it will be to explain how, when, and why your phenomenon unfolds and to generate categories that are rich, meaningful, and relevant to your goals.

After you have unitized and labeled your text, it is ideal if your labels are clear and succinct enough that you can begin to work with the unit labels rather than working with the original unit (but consulting the unit whenever needed to maintain clarity on its meaning). (In software, such as NVivo, the labels can be clicked on to reveal the unit of text, so they move together and remain connected as they are categorized.) For instance, when developing the label for the previously mentioned excerpt, an initial attempt might read, "When I was beginning my practicum, I thought it is scary not to have all the answers; I had learned from a past client that caring about clients helps them develop their own path because it helped her find a way forward." Removing words that do not answer the question of the interview or that are redundant can allow you to create a more succinct label. Also, if you use certain data processing software (e.g., NVivo, Atlas), you may have the external pressure of needing to keep your labels relatively short, so they can be easily seen on the screen. Because of this concern and for ease of comprehension in categorization, I usually try to keep labels no longer than 1.5 lines of text as a general rule.

Often, I find that my initial unit labels contain unnecessary words that can be removed fairly easily. The first unit, mentioned earlier, can be assigned an abbreviated label such as "Although it is scary not to have all the answers, I had learned that caring helps clients develop their own path." The second unit might receive a label such as "I learned that my own emotions cue me to how clients position themselves interpersonally with others." When coding interview transcripts, I will create meaning units within the Word document that contains my interview. I place them within square brackets at the end of each unit. This makes it easier for me to see the units within the transcript and copy and paste the labels into my software (see Example of Unitized and Labeled Text).

Keep the Unit Label Focused on Your Topic Rather Than Being Distracted by Asides or Idiosyncratic Detail

In my experience, beginning analysts tend to encounter three main challenges when creating meaning unit labels. First, they are tempted to create meaning units and labels that reflect their text but do not relate to the question driving the project. This can add irrelevant information into the analysis that will be distracting and hard to integrate, particularly if they had trouble keeping their interview on topic. For instance, if the research topic is the experience of grief, an interviewee might tell you about her father who passed:

> One thing I really enjoyed with my father was playing video games with him. There was this game that he really enjoyed called Zelda, in which he was a hero coming back to life after 100 years of being in a trance. You have to defeat all these monsters and magical beasts and recover lost memories to gain strength to defeat the evil dragon that had taken over the land. One time, we played together almost all night. We got so caught up because we kept thinking we were going to take over this magical beast, but then there would be another obstacle. I enjoyed how enthusiastic he was.

In this example, there are many details, but there is little about the experience of grief. You can imagine this description going on for much longer yet not containing more than is said in the label "an aspect of grief is missing enjoying connection and engagement with the person who is missed." If you code text describing details of the game, however, it will introduce material into the hierarchy that will not answer your study question and will be confusing.

Include Contextual Information

A second common problem is labeling units without providing the contextual information necessary to support its interpretation. For instance, if a unit in a study on cancer patients is labeled "Patients are afraid of hospitals," the reader does not know the context of the statement—which patients? What are they afraid of—the buildings, the doctors, the germs, the bureaucracy? Are they afraid in a certain stage of treatment? By including contextual information, it will be easier to see patterns in your data that will be obscured if you only use a few words for your unit titles. Contextual cues needed to create categories are clearer in the label "Patients are afraid that hospitals lead to contagion."

Centralize the Relevant Meaning

Another frequent challenge is labeling units in such a way that the larger meaning in a unit is not made clear. This issue occurs most often when a researcher is exploring the relationship between two phenomena. For instance, if a study focuses on the experience of being a woman construction worker, the focus of the interview and the meaning unit titles should describe the intersection of these two identities (e.g., "As a woman, I am less accepted by my fellow workers, and then I don't get offered as many opportunities"). If the relationship between these elements is disconnected into two meaning units (e.g., "I feel less accepted as a woman" and "At work, I don't get offered many opportunities"), the central meaning can be lost—the relationship between these ideas.

Use Evocative Language and Metaphors When Possible

It is helpful to keep your unit labels grounded in the language used by the participants. This practice will encourage you to be careful to read closely and not to veer too far from the meanings they are expressing. It is especially helpful to retain language that is especially evocative and metaphoric, alongside cues as to the context of its meaning. For instance, my all-time favorite study title came from a quote from participants in a study investigating religious leaders' thoughts about marital equality in the Southern United States: Anything with two heads is a monster (Levitt & Ware, 2006). These expressions can convey not only a literal meaning but also a web of associations that can deepen understanding, such as how this metaphor conveys the horror associated with relational equality.

At the same time, there may be occasions when a participant does not have the vocabulary to express what they mean or when you can use psychological terminology to describe their meaning more succinctly. It is okay to use your own phrases as long as you are cautious that your expression indeed does capture their meaning. Rennie and Fergus (2006) described the process of analysis as "embodied" because they noticed how the data made them feel, and they used their internal holistic sense of meaning to shape the labels to fit the data well. For example, in conducting research on butch lesbians, interviewees spoke over and over about wanting to be themselves, wanting to be who they are, and wanting to appear in a manner that reflected how they felt internally (Levitt & Hiestand, 2004). Although they did not use the term *authenticity*, this label fit well with the many stories that we heard and felt right to us. So, it can increase the fidelity of your analysis to use your own language when it captures the meanings more effectively than the participants' language while being sure that those labels are grounded in your sources' words.

Consider Signifying the Source of the Unit Before the Unit Label

Sometimes it will aid your analysis if you can look at the units within a category and see patterns in their origin (i.e., from which source or type of source they are derived). If you preface your meaning unit label with a code to indicate the participant or a key characteristic, it can help you more easily notice those patterns. For instance, when conducting a study on therapists, we were curious about whether therapists from across theoretical orientations would hold differing opinions about the therapy process (Levitt & Williams, 2010). To help with this, we typed "CBT" before units from cognitive behavior therapists, "HE" at the front of units from humanistic–existential therapists, "PP" to preface psychodynamic and psychoanalytic therapists' units, and "FM" before units from feminist–multicultural therapists. This process allowed us to easily look at our categories to see whether the meaning units they contained were disproportionately from one type of therapy or another. It allowed us to report on how the therapists differed and facilitated the identification of trends. You might have other distinctions you would like to track that are relevant to the questions you are asking. For instance, units might have come from interviewees in multiple countries or people in different stages of development, all of which could be tracked in this manner. This practice can be good to consider before you enter meaning units into your software.

Example of Unitized and Labeled Text

To help you visualize what these units look like in a transcript, the following dialogue is an excerpt from a mock interview on the process of developing therapeutic expertise. I often like to single space text and double space between speakers and bold the unit labels because it aids me in the visual reading of the transcript. I often type a sign (e.g., a tilde [~], see the example) to indicate which unit the label is reflecting. Here we reconsider a prior example.

INTERVIEWER (I): What was it like for you when you were just beginning to practice therapy?

PARTICIPANT (P): I remember having a moment where I was really scared during my first practicum. I was at home and ready to leave to catch the bus to the counseling center. I was already worried about being late because the bus was not so regular. And I thought, "What if I don't know how to help someone, and they become worse, and it's my fault?" I thought about my sister, though, and that kept me going. She had this terrible relationship, and her husband was insulting her all the time and cutting her off from her friends. Her husband had a job working in a software company, and he was working late all the time on this project to create voice-activated responses, but when he did see her, he was horrible. She wanted to leave the relationship, but she felt so alone. She told me afterwards that what I did that helped her the most was show that I cared about her and wanted her to be okay. It gave her the courage to keep caring about herself and to find a way out. So, I might not need to have all the answers, but I know how to support someone to find their own way. [~HL: **Although it is scary not to have all the answers, I had learned that caring about clients helps them develop their own path.**]

I: You felt you could support clients to find their own way. Did that idea help you?

P: Well, I felt less pressure to be the expert, and that was important for me when I really didn't feel like an expert yet. Also, I think it started me off remembering that it is really the clients' journey, and it isn't all about me. My job is to support them.

I: Where do you think that the fear of needing to be an expert came from?

P: Hmm. I guess it came in part from the media images of what it means to be a therapist, in movies, TV. I felt like I had to have this secret wisdom.

I: What do you mean when you say "secret wisdom"?

P: Well, when you see a therapist in the movies, they are usually quiet, and the client is talking and talking, and you wonder if they are even listening, but then all of a sudden, they say something that is brilliant, and it makes sense of everything the client has said and so much more.

[~**HL: I realized that I could support clients' journey, helping me overcome societal expectations that therapists have immediate answers.**] But also, I think it came from my practicum site. It was a short-term model of therapy, and the idea was to engage in these sets of manualized interventions. The emphasis was on learning those interventions and not as much on the process of forming a relationship or the process of supporting clients to form their own solutions. It focused my attention on learning interventions quickly so I could help them, and this made me think about therapy in a particular way.

I: Tell me more about how it made you think.

P: Well, it really helped me in that moment because I had strategies that I could work within, and this felt more secure to me, and the exercises did help the clients. Part of me thinks, though, that this focus delayed me from developing skills that would help clients to develop their own, personally, interpersonally, and culturally fitting solutions instead of relying on the exercises that I provided. The strategies helped me but didn't give me the basic skills that I craved. [~**HL: My practicum setting taught me manualized interventions, but the systemic values delayed my developing skills to support clients' self-direction.**]

I: How do you feel you came to learn those other therapy skills then?

P: I was in a program that wanted students to have a wide range of therapy skills, so I had a class in emotion-focused therapy, and I saw therapists tailoring what they did to their clients in a different way. This let me learn to be sensitive to the moment-to-moment process of therapy and to conceptualize the process of change as shifting all through the session as the client became more insightful or resistant or as they came to understand their feelings better and figure out what they needed to do. [~**HL: In emotion-focused class, I learned to understand the change process as shifting across the therapy session and how I could support clients where they were at.**] I didn't worry any longer about having an answer of what the client should do that would fix everything. Instead, I learned to help them see their emotional and relational patterns, and so they could figure out what they needed. [~**HL: Instead of trying to fix clients, I helped them see emotional and relational patterns so they could determine what they needed.**] It is important to me to continue learning therapy skills, and so I then sought out this learning actively by attending workshops, watching videos, and reading. [~**HL: Because I wanted to continue learning skills, I looked for reading, workshops, videos to learn more.**]

This transcript gives you a sense of how a unitized text might appear with unit labels inserted. Meaning units can be varied in length, however. Some units can be just a line or two, and other units can go on for a page or more, especially when participants are relaying stories to exemplify points they are making. I tend to find that an average unit is about a half page in length.

CONSTANT COMPARISON AND THE CREATION OF INITIAL CATEGORIES

After you have created meaning units from about three or four interviews (or a similar amount of data from other sources), you might begin to create categories. Beginning the process before all your data are collected is typical of grounded theory methods because it will give you a sense of gaps in your data and lead you to consider the sorts of participants to recruit via theoretical sampling (see Chapter 4). Before you begin the process of constant comparison, it is helpful to keep a record of how many meaning units were created from your project (i.e., copy each into a separate folder in your software program) so you can report that number when you describe your analysis so that readers understand your analytic process.

Some approaches to grounded theory (e.g., *axial coding* in Strauss & Corbin's, 1998, version) label their initial units with a word or short phrase (e.g., in a study on the process of transference analysis, "projective defense mechanisms"; in a study on internalized stigma, "origin of internalized heterosexism") and then identify the related processes, action or interaction strategies, conditions, and consequences. In contrast, I recommend conceptualizing categories as sentences that capture the processes, functions, and contexts described in the unit titles. The continued focus on the information in the unit that is meaningful in relation to your research question prevents the researcher from spending time establishing a plethora of overly fragmented observations that are challenging to synthesize. Instead, the processes and relationships relevant to your question are centralized throughout the analytic process.

Constant Comparison

In the process of constant comparison, researchers compare each unit with every other unit to generate categories that capture common meanings. This process is conducted by looking primarily at the labels you have assigned to the units and referring to the actual unit whenever necessary to gain clarification on what was said. For example, from the interview about learning therapy, you have an initial list of unit labels such as this:

1. Although it is scary not to have all the answers, I had learned that caring about clients helps them develop their own path.

2. I realized that I could support clients' journeys, helping me overcome societal expectations that therapists have immediate answers.

3. My practicum setting taught me manualized interventions, but the systemic values delayed my developing skills to support clients' self-direction.

4. In emotion-focused class, I learned to understand the change process as shifting across the therapy session and how I could support clients where they were at.

5. Instead of trying to fix clients, I helped them see emotional and relational patterns so they could determine what they needed.

6. Because I wanted to continue learning skills, I looked for reading, workshops, and videos to learn more.

I would begin with Unit Label 1 and compare it with each other unit label, referring back to the units themselves as is helpful. If I find multiple connections between units, it is okay because units can be placed in more than one category. If you refer back to these units, you can follow along to see the steps I would take when engaging in constant comparison with these units:

- Comparing Units 1 and 2. These unit labels both seem to address the worry around expertise. I would think about the commonality between them and place them together in Category 1: "I can resist social pressure to have ready answers because I can support clients to develop their own path via a caring relationship." In this comparison, I can see the personal and social sphere intersecting in the construction of meaning. Higher order categories may develop this idea in a more theoretical manner later, but I want to capture the initial formulation in this category to provide the ground for that later analysis.

- Comparing Units 1 and 3. These two units seem connected in that they both refer to self-direction, though one refers to not having answers and one to providing answers. Because the unit label for Unit 3 does not make clear whether manualized interventions reduced the sense of anxiety, I looked back at the unit text to find that they did increase security. This helps me to represent both the content and process of meaning creation. Then I would place the units in a new Category 2: "Manualized interventions were less scary because they supplied answers, but they blocked my goal of learning to guide clients' self-direction."

- Comparing Units 1, 2, and 3. When I reflect on Units 1, 2, and 3 with a critical lens, I see that the text indicates power in society and the participant's practicum setting that appears to be converging to create a systems-level expectation—that therapists should provide quick answers, guided by preestablished interventions. I might call this category "Dominant discourses at practica and society focused on short-term preset interventions, keeping her from seeking the skills she desires to support clients' self-determination." Although initially, category labels might seem close to the content of the units, as more units are added to your category, the title will naturally become conceptually more abstract to reflect the commonalities therein. For instance, a later title might become "The economics of therapy has led the field to discard the goal of client self-determination."

- Comparing Units 1 and 4. Here, I see some connection in the phrase "I learned to understand," which implies that the change process was now conceptualized differently. A category title might be "I shifted from conceptualizing change as resulting from an answer to seeing it as an evolving process of supporting clients' growth." In this way, you can capture changes across time in your data by noting shifts in participants' meaning.

- Comparing Units 1 and 5. I see the commonality between the first unit and Unit 5 as being quite similar to the commonality we identified between Unit 1 and Unit 3. For this reason, I would add the unit to Category 2. To better capture the content of this unit, I would tweak the unit title so that it now reads, "I am not scared to support clients to identify their own patterns and develop their own path in a caring relationship."

- Comparing Units 1 and 6. I do not see a commonality between Unit 1 and 6, so I would skip over to examining the next meaning unit label. Typically, most of your units will have meanings that are discrete from most other units, so this practice will be common.

This process of comparison will continue across the unit labels (e.g., taking Label 2 to compare with all units below it, then Label 3). Initially, this process will take a great deal of work because almost every comparison will result in the conceptualization and creation of a new category. As more and more categories are formed, you will find that more units will fall into existing categories, and the process will not be as intensive.

Tips on Creating Initial Categories

Many of the tips given for creating meaning unit labels hold for creating categories. For instance, it is helpful to have category titles that are focused on the central study concern, provide enough context to be useful, contain meaningful content, and include evocative language when possible. The following are common errors that I have found myself and others making when initially forming categories. Being aware of them can help you to create stronger categories. It also can be helpful to review your hierarchy periodically and examine your categories for these sorts of problems.

Avoid Having Two Categories That Share the Same Meaning

Because people can word similar ideas in many ways, it is not unusual that categories may be created that are expressing the same meaning. For instance, in a study of queer participants, they may talk about how they want to be visible as queer and how they do not want to pass as heterosexual, citing similar reasons. Your hierarchy will become cumbersome if it contains multiple copies of the same idea, so when you have categories expressing the same idea, it is best to combine them (e.g., Being seen as queer is important for Reasons X and Y).

Avoid Creating Categories That Reflect Your Questions Instead of Answers

It is unfortunately quite common to have findings of grounded theory studies in which the results are a reworking of the questions asked (Timulak & Elliott, 2018). This is probably the most common error that I see when reviewing qualitative methods. For instance, a paper might include questions such as How do people understand injustice? When do people feel injustice? How does injustice affect people? If the categories in the resulting paper are "Understandings of injustice," "Times people feel injustice," and "Influences of injustice," you can see that they are a reformulation of the question asked. They do not provide any information at all about the answers to the questions being asked. Instead, the analysts are leaving it to the reader to read the content within the results section and try to organize it into an answer themselves, when it is the analysts' place to do this work because they are the ones who have had complete access to the data and have studied it.

Avoid Polarized Categories

Although it will make your hierarchy challenging to code if categories are too similar, you also do not want to have contradictory categories. If one category reads, "I don't like being a teacher," and another reads, "I like being a teacher," the reader will not understand how to reconcile these differing opinions or make use of the results. It is better to consider when one stance might hold and when another might hold and represent these in a combined category. For instance, a combined category label might be "I usually like teaching, except I don't enjoy grading" or "I like teaching students, but I don't like having few of the supports that I need to do this well" or "I like teaching when I am in a supportive school context but not when I am not." In that way, the reader will know when to draw on one set of findings and when to draw on the other. It can be helpful to consider terms that can structure these relationships, such as *when, except, but, after, usually, because, while,* and *although.* When you identify contradictory ideas within your data, it can be an exciting creative time as you conceptualize how best to draw forth the idea that might underlie that difference and seek coherences.

Have a Longer, Meaningful Category Title Rather Than a Concise One That Is Hard to Interpret

A category title should be as long as it needs to be to convey the meaning therein with fidelity. If researchers try to form category titles that mimic the names of factors (e.g., "Tensions in my relationship"), it may be hard for other analysts to interpret what it means (what tensions?). Providing contextual details will make your category clearer (e.g., "Experiencing workplace harassment adds tension to my romantic relationship"). In contrast, a short category title may completely capture the idea within a category and usefully push the field ahead. The main question to ask yourself is what is needed to describe the concept with fidelity and what will be useful with regard to your study aims.

Look for Subcategories That Can Inform Your Category Title

As you form a hierarchy, you may find that some categories contain long lists of meaning units within them. I often use a heuristic in which when there are more than six meaning units, I will check the list of units to see whether subcategories can be made to more finely draw out distinctions within the data. Sometimes this may not be the case because all the units say the same thing. Other times, however, subcategories can be created. This practice is useful because it allows you to both develop a better organization of subcategories and fine-tune the name of the category title above them. If I am able to refine a category title, I will examine all the categories above that to see whether their titles require adjustment as well after this newfound clarity.

Creating Upper Level Categories

To maintain clarity about the levels of categories that I am creating, I usually specify a set of terminology (see Figure 5.1). As indicated before, I use the

FIGURE 5.1. Terminology to Describe Hierarchy Levels

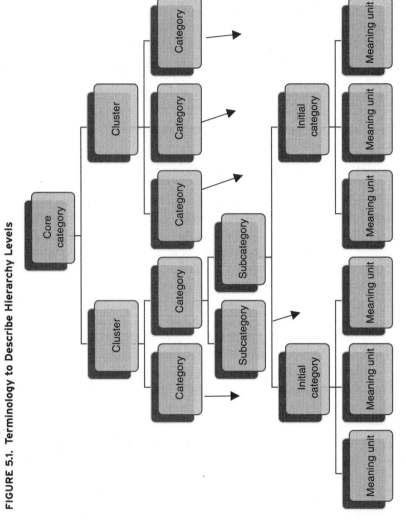

Note. Arrows indicate that lower levels of categories would continue from points that are not shown here.

term *initial categories* to refer to the categories created from the meaning units. For the top three levels of the hierarchy, I use the following terms: The *core category* is at the apex of the hierarchy, *clusters* are the categories that are on the level just beneath it, and *categories* refers to the level beneath that. There may be additional levels of *subcategories* between these categories and the initial categories, but hierarchies often just have these four levels of categories.

Because the upper levels contain the levels below them, it is usually sufficient to describe the three top levels in presenting findings. In an article, it also would be unusual to refer to more than these three levels because of page length restrictions. If your data generate more layers of the hierarchy between the initial categories and these three layers, they would be formed by following the same processes described here for the upper level categories.

Tips on Creating Higher Level Categories

I find three additional guidelines are helpful when creating higher level categories.

Categories Should Contain Either Subcategories or Meaning Units

When you are in the process of analyzing your data, it will help you to keep meaning units and category titles organized so that categories encompass either meaning units (if they are initial categories) or subcategories (if they are higher order categories) rather than having meaning units and subcategories mixed together within categories throughout your hierarchy. When these are mixed together, it will be harder to see the concepts driving your higher order categories, and it will become confusing to read. If they become mixed together, it will be worthwhile to take some time to organize them because this process will help you examine subcategories side by side, which will allow you to sharpen the label of the higher category that subsumes them.

Avoid Creating Higher Order Category Labels That List Properties

Another challenge that researchers face, especially when developing labels for higher order categories, is the temptation to generate a list of the ideas in the categories below rather than to identify the commonalities between those categories. For instance, in a study on the experiences of being an activist, you might develop the following category labels that describe participants' experience before activism:

- I feel ashamed that I did not recognize sexism before working at the shelter.
- I even doubted statistics about domestic violence in my country.

I questioned the purpose of feminism and did not claim this identity then. A researcher might examine these categories and form a higher order category labeled "Before activism, I did not recognize sexism, doubted domestic violence statistics, and questioned feminism." This sort of label does capture the experiences in the initial categories, but it does not engage in the conceptual work of the analysis. Instead, if you considered the commonality that holds these categories together, you might form a more conceptually powerful category: "Activism often corrects a history of denying oppression." By identifying the common concept underlying the initial categories, readers can better understand the dynamic being described and consider its broader implications for training or other ways to use the findings.

Consider the Number of Clusters and Categories as You Plan to Publish

A pragmatic issue to consider when developing your hierarchy is how many clusters and categories you will be able to report on in your article. If you have too many, you will not be able to describe them all within a single journal-length manuscript. The number will depend in part on your data and the number of clusters needed to describe it with fidelity, but it can be useful to consider the journals to which you submit, and whether they have page restrictions, as you plan. Depending on your goals for your project and the way your analysis proceeds, you might decide that a book is a better outlet for your work, a journal without a stringent page restriction is a better place to publish, or your findings should be reported in multiple articles. If you report on parts of a hierarchy that answer distinctive subquestions, it is not a piecemeal publication. When developing a single manuscript from the article, I try to have as few clusters (the level beneath the core category) as possible so that I have space to describe each cluster with some depth—most typically between three and seven. I consider the numbers of categories within in cluster as well and tend to avoid having more than four or five categories in a cluster (it becomes harder for readers to retain the cluster theme in mind). Also, if you have fewer clusters, you will have space to describe more categories within them, so this can encourage you to combine categories and clusters that are overly similar to give you more room for depth of explanation. Ultimately, though, you should be guided in the analytic process to represent your data with fidelity, so your findings are clear to readers. More on this issue and how the concern around piecemeal publications applies to qualitative research is discussed in Chapter 6 on writing a manuscript.

Creating a Core Category

Your core category should emerge from considering the common ideas across your uppermost level of categories, your clusters. Because it captures the central idea in your analysis and organizes how people understand the rest of the hierarchy, it is probably the category on which you will spend the most time. This process of developing a core category (and relating higher order categories to it) is akin to Strauss and Corbin's (1998) process of selective coding. I describe here the processes used in a critical-constructivist method.

A good core category benefits from having both fidelity and utility. First, it will capture an idea that you think will improve the understanding of your phenomenon. It should encourage readers to see the dynamics in and between the clusters more completely than they had before. Sometimes the core category does this by drawing out one concept that transforms how an idea is understood, such as how "negotiating credibility" casts a new light on the process of journals' peer review (Oddli et al., 2017, p. 5). At other times, the core category can develop a new understanding of a chain of events, such as this core category from a grounded theory meta-analysis of clients' experiences: "Being known and cared for supports clients' ability to agentically recognize obstructive experiential patterns and address unmet vulnerable needs" (Levitt et al., 2016, p. 348). The core category centralizes clients' agency in recognizing their patterns and needs and frames the therapist as ancillary to that activity, generating an understanding of therapy rooted in the client's perspective.

Second, a core category should be useful by meeting the goals for your research project. It should be innovative and introduce solutions that are new to the field. If the core category communicates something that seems to strongly reflect your data (i.e., it has fidelity) but says something that has been written about a million times before, it will not have utility, and readers will not find your study interesting. For instance, finding that psychotherapy clients benefit from having a strong alliance with their therapist is accurate, but it has been written about so extensively that most readers will not learn anything new from reading your paper. It can be better to draw forward what is innovative about your findings and in your specific context.

Although grounded theory analyses typically result in core categories, it may be that you realize in your analysis that a core category does not make sense for your hierarchy. In that case, it will make sense to stop your hierarchy at the cluster level. For instance, let's say that the main finding of your study is that people from different countries do not have the same idea of what it means to be polite. In that case, you might decide that to create a core category will only misrepresent the main finding by suggesting that there is a core concept. Your study might have greater fidelity by developing a hierarchy without a core category (because having a category that says "there is no common pattern" is tantamount to saying that there is no core category).

INFERENTIAL PROCESSES UNDERLYING THE CREATION OF THE HIERARCHY

The process of developing a hierarchy in grounded theory has been understood as rooted in a cycle of inferential processes by which researchers gradually refine their findings through an iterative process of analysis. Understanding this process can help you better explain this method to others (and defend qualitative methods generally). Rennie (2000, 2012) described *methodical hermeneutics* as a cycle involving four inferential processes.

These processes can be summarized as (a) *eduction*, drawing forth what seems meaningful about a piece or section of data by reflecting on it in light of the researchers' experiences and knowledge about what is important (e.g., by creating a meaning unit); (b) *abduction*, formulating an approximation of the inherent meaning by considering what might efficiently explain the data (e.g., by generating a label for that unit); (c) *theorematic deduction*, deciding that continued analysis could provide useful evidence (i.e., by selecting a new unit to examine or new data source); and (d) *induction*, seeking out commonalities across data to see whether they consistently explain the patterns observed and making adjustments to establish a fitting conceptualization (e.g., by generating categories).

After developing an initial conceptualization of a section of data (e.g., a category), the cycle begins again with new units being considered. Moving through these stages gradually shifts the meaning generated to reflect more and more of the variation in the phenomenon under study (Levitt, in press) and eventually leads to a comprehensive theory (e.g., saturation). In this way, the analysis itself incorporates a self-correcting process. Other researchers also have identified the hermeneutic process as a key way that meaning is generated across qualitative methods (e.g., Levitt et al., 2018; Osbeck, 2014).

INCORPORATING A CRITICAL-CONSTRUCTIVIST LENS IN CATEGORIZATION

Through much of this chapter, the use of a critical-constructivist lens is embedded in the description of procedures and examples. Although I provided a general overview of constructivist and critical epistemological approaches in Chapter 1, there is no way that I can review even a small fraction of all the constructivist and critical theories that you can bring to bear when engaging in your analysis. I do recommend reading within whatever framework you have selected to use before you begin the process of both data collection and analysis so you are better able to engage in these perspectives.

Common to these theories is a concern with examining the interpersonal processes of developing meaning and social practices (constructivist approaches) and a related concern with how social power dynamics influence meaning and practices (critical approaches). Another shared concern is that researchers should not focus only on the commonalities within their findings and flatten out important differences between the varied social realities, social systems, and stressors within the participants in your analysis. You may notice a realist-postmodern tension (Bettez, 2015) in shaping a balance between representing patterns of similarity and difference. The concepts of fidelity and utility can guide you. Although descriptions of commonality will help the reader understand the central patterns, the contexts, processes, and actions associated with difference are necessary for an accurate description of your findings and to direct readers to apply them appropriately. In this section, I explicate strategies that can sensitize you to these ideas through your analysis and help you identify the discourses implicit in your data.

Consider Multiple Social Spheres

It can be helpful to consider how the participants are socially situated in multiple contexts that are influenced by one another within your analysis. To facilitate your conceptualization of these spheres, you might decide to use mapping techniques such as diagrams (Glaser & Strauss, 1967) or conditional matrices (Strauss & Corbin, 1990). *Situational analysis* (Clarke, 2009) is an approach to grounded theory that guides researchers to use empirical evidence to develop situational maps of elements related to the situation of inquiry, positional maps of the bipolar conceptual variations related to an issue, and maps of the social world or arena surrounding a phenomenon (e.g., personal, community, organization, national, international arena). This approach provides a structure that can support researchers to develop an understanding of how human, material, and discursive elements interact. These mapping techniques are especially useful for sociological, systemic, or ecological research because they center on helping researchers examine the layers in which phenomena unfold (e.g., see Grzanka, 2020; Jacobson et al., 2013). For psychological research or research on subjective experience, I see these as helpful adjunctive exercises that can facilitate critical perspectives, especially for novice researchers new to thinking critically.

Consider Change Across Historical Epoch, Place, and Time

Expectations and histories of oppression may continue to act subtly or intergenerationally. The people who originally developed a certain discourse may not even exist any longer, and that discourse can still lead to expectations influencing groups today. Consider not just the discourse but who benefitted originally from that discourse and who benefits now. These questions are especially useful for research that is concerned with anthropological or historical meaning or is examining a concept that has held meaning that has evolved intergenerationally. For instance, in my analysis of gender, I present a set of grounded theory studies focused on how masculinities and femininities evolved in lesbian, gay, bisexual, transgender, and queer (LGBTQ+) communities within the United States. The findings reflect layers of meanings influenced by national historical events, such as war and economics; national issues, such as health care and human rights; and local dynamics that unfolded within LGBTQ+ communities at specific times and sociocultural moments.

Consider Multiple Perspectives

It can advance your research to consider the vantage point of people located in varied positions with respect to your phenomena. For instance, a study on treatment might include, as participants or within an advisory team, therapists, clients, clients' family members, insurance agencies, and legislators. Even when studying participants who occupy one perspective, you might contemplate or ask questions about how their perspectives would shift if they were in another socioeconomic or demographic group. You could consider the experience of those who are oppressed, those who are oppressive, and those who are bystanders to develop more insight into how expectations, meanings, and power is structured, enforced, and communicated. For instance, in a multilevel project on intimate partner violence within faith communities, we conducted separate analyses of survivors, perpetrators, and religious leaders to describe how religion could promote and prevent violence (e.g., Levitt & Ware, 2006). As you generate units and categories and shape your hierarchy, I encourage you to incorporate these strategies because they will further the fidelity and utility of your findings. In the next sections, I describe the concrete process of moving through these steps and provide examples.

Consider the Role of Symbolic Items and Actions Within Your Data

As you conceptualize how participants and their social systems interact with the phenomenon you are studying, it will help to notice the symbols that are constructed in the participants' process of meaning making. For instance, sense of identity or affiliation with a community can be influenced by signs, symbols, and objects specific to that group (e.g., in the LGBTQ+ leather community, these might include flags, leather garb, and rituals; Levitt, 2019). Signifiers of an idea can come to represent an identity, a concept, or a dynamic. Then, they facilitate communication by signaling to others the sets of values, beliefs, or positions held by a person or group. Symbolic items or activities may function by constructing meanings that are interpersonally meaningful or culturally oppressive or subversive.

THE PROCESS OF HIERARCHY REVIEW

As you are developing your hierarchy, you will want to periodically review your categories and clean them up by merging redundant ones, creating subcategories as needed, and refining the labels of the categories. Over time, as you are entering the units from your interviews into the hierarchy, you will notice that fewer and fewer categories need to be created. This is because most of the ideas associated with your topic have already been organized into categories. This is a sign that you are approaching saturation. At this moment, it is wise to halt the process of adding new data into the hierarchy and conduct a close review to clean up redundancies, differentiate overly similar category titles, and ensure that your meaning units and categories appear on separate levels in the hierarchy (i.e., not mixed up) so that all your data are well organized and has had the chance to influence the developing conceptualization.

This review will often require you to review the hierarchy from the initial categories upward, reconsidering each of the meaning units and checking that they are placed within the categories that are relevant to them. Often, in this process, I create many subcategories that help me refine my category titles (which, in turn, help me refine the higher order category titles). Through this process, I keep in mind the challenge of how to emphasize features in the hierarchy that improve the current understanding of the nature of my topic (i.e., its fidelity) and that will be useful, given the goals of the project (i.e., its utility). It is a creative and edifying experience and results in a tighter hierarchy that is more likely to reach saturation (more in the next section).

METHODOLOGICAL INTEGRITY CHECKS

Qualitative researchers will sometimes add additional checks to their studies to improve the methodological integrity of their studies. Because qualitative analyses are inherently self-correcting (Rennie, 2012), these checks often are supplementary to the rigor that is already central in the analytic process. This said, the practices of saturation and memoing are intrinsic to the conceptualization of grounded theory methods (Glaser & Strauss, 1967), so they typically will be an expected aspect of this method.

Saturation

After I have completed the hierarchy review, I will begin tracking the process of adding data from new sources to my hierarchy to see when saturation is reached. *Saturation* is the point in an analysis when the addition of new data no longer results in the creation of new categories and ideas in your hierarchy (Glaser & Strauss, 1967). Researchers will use differing thresholds to establish saturation, and you will want to describe whether and how you experienced the process of your understanding solidifying (Braun & Clarke, 2019). Although you may continue to tweak phrasing of category titles and reorganize them up until publication, your data being saturated suggests that incoming data seems redundant and your hierarchy is comprehensive, so your data collection can cease. Typically, if I am conducting hour-long interviews, I feel more confident about saturation when at least two interviews did not result in new categories. If I am working with shorter excerpts, such as answers from survey questions or meta-analyses, I will increase this number because each source has fewer units and is less of a test of saturation. I will use a saturation log, such as the one in Table 5.1, to assist in tracking this process.

Participant Feedback or Member Checking

Seeking participant feedback or member checking (synonyms for the same process) can help provide you with information on how well your findings mesh with the experiences of those whom you interviewed. This process is illuminating because it can increase your confidence about your work, allow

TABLE 5.1. Saturation Log

Date	Interview number	Name of new category	Level of the hierarchy from bottom
01-06-20	10	Supervisor as a model of how to intervene	5
01-15-20	11	Therapy as continual experiment	6
01-20-20	12	No new categories	—

you to correct places where you have gone astray, help you revise your findings to become more inclusive, and guide you to present findings with appropriate descriptions of their applicability.

Not all grounded theorists seek participant feedback. There are times when it will not make sense to seek participant feedback on your findings (Motulsky, 2019). For instance, if the topic you are studying is largely outside of the participants' awareness, they will not be able to give you useful feedback. For instance, if you are analyzing unconscious processes, such as transference, a defining aspect of that phenomenon is that it occurs out of awareness. Or, if you are studying the influence of larger social processes, such as systemic racism, participants may not be aware of the many guises this can take because it is normalized in society. In those cases, feedback may not be desirable or necessary, and any feedback gathered should be understood within these limitations. At other times, participant feedback may be difficult or inappropriate when the subject of the study is so painful that it would cause the participants considerable distress to review the findings; when participants have a high level of life stress, and their original contribution to research is all they can provide; when they are reluctant to participate in research; or when they are transient and it would be challenging to locate them for feedback. In these situations, there may be ethical issues to consider (Motulsky, 2019). From a social justice perspective, it is more important to have their voices represented in the literature than to restrict this because of an interest in obtaining supplemental feedback.

Because the approach to grounded theory that I advocate is located within a critical-constructivist approach, I do not consider the process of gathering feedback to be a process of checking the objectivity of my conceptualization (e.g., the idea that there is one experience that everyone should agree on). Instead, I am using feedback to learn about the limitations of the conceptualization that I am proposing and how it differs from people's perspectives (constructivist idea) and their social situations (critical idea). In this process, I am not as interested in points of agreement (although these can be affirming) but in learning when and how my conceptualization might need either revision or qualification to better fit with my participants' diverse experiences. While the participants have authority on their own individual experiences, as a researcher, you seek to reflect all of the participants' experiences. This means that feedback from one participant does not automatically veto the understandings you have developed, but you should consider how best to integrate it within or alongside your data.

Also, I understand the feedback process in relation to the feminist understanding of epistemic privilege (e.g., Code, 1993; Harding, 2015; see

Chapter 2, this volume, for a description). Each participant provides feedback from their own experiences and the situated knowledge they have accrued, so I use the process as a critical participatory element of the design that is shaping and informing the final findings. This feedback can help investigators move beyond the limits of their cultural understanding. Typically, because the results are grounded in participants' accounts, feedback should not produce stark discrepancies, but you often will find that you receive important clarifications or qualifications on your findings that can help you in conceptualizing and reporting findings so they speak across cultural perspectives. For instance, in a study on navigating transgender minority stress (Levitt & Ippolito, 2014), feedback from participants indicated that the workplace minority stress we described had dissipated once they found affirming work environments. As a result, we described this feedback in our article.

Similarly, if you have conflicting feedback, you can report that a result seemed to fit more for participants with one characteristic than another. Your goal is to reconcile the feedback and transparently present the differences across participants in relation to the information that you have learned about their context, beliefs, and positions. This information later will guide the transferability of your findings (Lincoln & Guba, 1985).

Teamwork and Consensus in Critical-Constructivist Grounded Theory Methods

Psychological researchers who are conducting grounded theory research within a team setting often will use a process of group consensus, although it is not part of the original grounded theory method. There are varied rationales and aims for using consensus (e.g., Hill, 2012). From a postpositivist perspective, establishing consensus across a team is a way to demonstrate that the findings can be seen by multiple people, increasing the sense that the analysis is accessing an objective reality. In a critical-constructivist approach to grounded theory, consensus is used to serve both constructivist and critical aims (Levitt, Morrill, et al., in press). From a constructivist perspective, consensus is used to heighten researchers' sensitivity to varied ways of making sense of the data, which can deepen the understanding of the meanings attributed to a concept. From a critical perspective, consensus ensures that the perspectives of people from varied positions of power are considered.

Critical researchers also often choose to engage in power sharing, using participatory designs (Teo, 2015) to determine their research scope and agenda. To create a participatory grounded theory design, you might invite research team members who vary in their positionality in relation to your topic to work with you to shape your study goals and design, assist in the interpretation of your data, or consider ways to apply your findings (see Levitt, 2019; Parker, 2015). These collaborations can be productive because they can generate new insights.

Often, if we are studying a group, we strive to include research team members who are affiliated with that group (e.g., butch and femme lesbian coanalysts studying butch gender; Levitt & Hiestand, 2004) because they will bring an insider's perspective to that experience and a lived experience that can enrich understanding on a variety of levels, and we seek feedback on findings from that community. At the same time, nongroup members can help with considering what would be most useful for nongroup members to understand when considering the labeling of higher order categories and the writing of the paper. Having both perspectives in a team can lead to rich discussions on how best to communicate findings. In addition to considering in- and outgroup members, the researchers may wish to involve other stakeholders who have a role in how power is enacted within the issue under study (e.g., Fine, 2013). For instance, you might engage a consultation team of therapists, patients, and nurses to guide and provide feedback on research in a hospital treatment program.

Dividing Teamwork

When dividing up labor within a critical-constructivist approach to grounded theory methods, you might consider how to maximize the use of the team members' expertise across the various tasks. For instance, if it is possible to have the interviewers create the meaning units within their interviews, it can be advantageous in that they bring with them the lived experience of that interview, and other things being equal, they may have a deeper sense of the meaning in that interview. Also, if you have separate people conducting the interviews, it can be beneficial for them to summarize the main ideas that they learned from the interviews and their experience of interviewing so that nonverbal information can be conveyed to the larger team.

In the process of analyzing the interviews, I often have researchers begin by creating units and initial categories within their own interviews and obtaining feedback from a team member and me before they go on to create categories by comparing their interviews with other data sources in the project. After their initial process of creating units and categories is approved, researchers, either individually or in small groups, can go on to conduct constant comparison by comparing their meaning units with those of the others in the project. In using this structure, I recommend that researchers memo the changes they make to the hierarchy so they can describe them and any questions that arose in team meetings. Then, the larger group can consider and discuss the changes. As you move to create the higher order categories, you may find it beneficial to develop findings in the context of the entire team so all the diverse forms of expertise and perspectives are brought to bear (see Chapter 2 on epistemic privilege).

Feedback and Hierarchy Review Within Teamwork

Throughout this process, it will be important to provide regular feedback to the work of all members of the team so that everyone is on the same page. When I am in working in the capacity of being the team leader, I usually give feedback to team members after each of the first two or three interviews, after the initial creation of meaning units on one or two transcripts, after the formation of initial categories on one or two transcripts, as they shift to form higher order categories, and as they begin to conceptualize a core category. If members will be continuing to conduct analyses independently, I will give them feedback until I judge that they are ready to do so, so the amount of material that I review is specific to the needs of each team member.

Also, within this structure, the person giving feedback is typically the primary author or principal investigator of the grounded theory project because of the time investment that this can take to do well. Because they are reviewing and guiding the generation of all the interviews, the creation of the meaning units and initial categories, and the process of creating the hierarchy, they become intimately familiar with the project. This person often engages in the process of reviewing the hierarchy as well (see the previous section of this chapter describing the hierarchy review process). This familiarity positions them to serve in the capacity of an internal auditor (Lincoln & Guba, 1985)—that is, someone from the research team who conducts a close review of the hierarchy, providing feedback to the research team to consider but who also is a driving member of the analysis by participating in the team. An advantage of this approach to organizing a team is that it maintains the deep knowledge of all the data by a central member while benefiting from the diversity of expertise and perspectives that a team can provide.

Qualitative Software

You may wish to use software to help you analyze your data (e.g., NVivo, ATLAS; see Woods et al., 2016, for details). Software does make the data easier to organize, but it is not necessary. The main advantage of software programs is that they allow you to more easily drag and drop units and categories beneath each other and pull up the text associated with a meaning unit label with less effort. If they are not available, you can also conduct a grounded theory analysis using a word processor (see the following example). To do this, you will

1. Create and track data by adding line numbering into your transcripts to create units.

2. Use these line numbers to create and track meaning units and then assign labels to them and unit numbers (which will be used in the next step, indicating the transcript number is also helpful).

3. Use these unit numbers to help you sort the meaning units into categories (now assigning category numbers to them).

4. Use the category numbers to organize categories into higher order categories in a similar manner.

The following example of these steps may be helpful for you.

EXAMPLE OF USING A WORD PROCESSOR TO CONDUCT ANALYSIS

1. Add transcript line numbers. You do not usually have to type line numbers into the transcript. Word processors can add them automatically—just set it so that numbering is continuous and does not begin again on each page, and you can create tables, such as the ones in this example, to track the formation of meaning units, initial categories, and higher order categories.

2. Use the line numbers in the transcript to locate meaning units. Then create labels for the units. Number the meaning units so you can create initial categories using these numbers in the next step (e.g., Transcript 01-Unit 01 = T1-01).

Transcript, Line # Transcript and Meaning Unit #, and Unit Label

T1, 1-20 T1-01 My racial identity helps me understand who I am and my history

T1, 21-29 T1-02 My racial identity helps me feel more confident about my strengths, even when they differ from other people

T1, 30-75 T1-03 My racial identity lets me be more assertive and confident

T2, 1-19 T2-01 My racial identity supports me to stand up for my political beliefs

3. Organize the unit numbers to group units into categories and then assign a category label. Then, assign a number to that category (e.g., Category-01 = C-01).

Category Units Initial Category # and Category Label

T1-01, T1-02, T1-03 C-01 My racial identity allows me to communicate and prize my own experiences

T1-03, T2-01 C-02 My racial identity promotes political activism

T1-01, T1-02 C-03 My racial identity allows for greater self-understanding and acceptance

T1-07, T1-11 C-04 Having a group helps you feel better when discriminated against

4. Organize the category numbers to show your formation of higher order categories. Then, assign numbers to these higher order categories and continue your analysis in this manner.

Initial Category # Higher Order Category # and Higher Order Category Label

C-01, C-03 HC-01 My racial identity increases my self-esteem by increasing my political awareness

C-02, C-04, C-11 HC-02 Inherent in a racial identity are tools to resist oppression

C-05, C-09, C-01 HC-03 My relationships are strengthened by a more complex understanding of race

AGGREGATING GROUNDED THEORY STUDIES: GROUNDED THEORY META-ANALYSIS

Although our focus is on primary research papers in which authors present their own analyses, innovative approaches have been developed to review the primary research in an area. Glaser (2013) clarified the difference between substantive grounded theory and formal grounded theory—the latter extends the general implications of core categories across an area of research (see Kearney, 2001, for details). In these meta-analyses, the results of primary grounded theories are each converted into meaning units and then subjected to a grounded theory analysis. These meta-analyses (sometimes called metasyntheses) condense research and identify trends in findings that are especially robust because they hold across varied studies. The goal of these approaches is to create findings that extend across the particularities of individual studies in an area of research. There are growing numbers of examples in psychology of these studies (e.g., Levitt et al., 2016; Timulak, 2009).

6

WRITING A MANUSCRIPT

Recently, a task force of the American Psychological Association generated the inaugural set of standards for reporting qualitative research (see Levitt et al., 2018, for complete details). These outlined the elements that should be included in qualitative manuscripts broadly. This chapter reviews the central ways that writing a manuscript describing a grounded theory study are distinctive from writing a quantitative manuscript or a general qualitative study. I review the sections of a typical grounded theory paper and provide a template to help you structure your papers.

A central difference in writing qualitative manuscripts is that it is typical that authors will use the first person in describing their research process throughout their paper. Describing who you are, your positionality with respect to your topic, and how you changed in the research process can bring the readers along with you on your research journey. It can be useful, however, to examine the tradition of the journal to which you wish to submit to decide how much detail about your process might be welcomed and how formal a tone is expected in that outlet. How important that journal audience is to you may inform the degree of risk you decide to adopt to report your research in a style that is comfortable to you.

https://doi.org/10.1037/0000231-006

INTRODUCTION

Like most manuscripts, the Introduction section for a grounded theory paper will frame the problem by describing its contemporary understanding. Usually, this process entails reviewing the research relevant to the central research question (make this question clear!). The goal of this review is to establish the need for your study and how it might contribute to the state of knowledge, correct misunderstandings, and fill knowledge gaps. It is typically good form to value the contributions that have come before yours and, instead of savagely critiquing past problems, to indicate how your work can build on what has come before.

Because you will be proposing a grounded theory study, typically, you will want to argue that a new conceptualization of your phenomenon will advance the field in some way. For instance, it might suggest new treatment, develop sensitivity that can enhance clinical practice or education, or help shape policy initiatives. It can be helpful to identify the two or three reasons that you believe that a new conceptualization is needed and then shape the subsections of your introduction around these ideas. Introduction sections in grounded theory analyses are typically quite short because more space is needed in the methods and discussion. Usually, at the end of the Introduction section, there is a section describing your research aims. There, researchers often briefly describe the epistemological framework within which they are working to situate their research goals and their approach to conceptualizing their method. Within a 35-page manuscript, about six to seven pages is a typical length.

METHOD

Because there are many versions of grounded theory, it will help to specify the version that you are using (e.g., critical-constructivist) and add a brief description and/or citations so that your reader understands the approach. Within a 35-page manuscript, the Method section is about five to seven pages in length.

Participants

Your Participants section will include information on your data sources or interviewees (e.g., demographic information and other information relevant to their selection or context) and also information about the researcher(s) as well. When describing the researcher(s), you will want to describe aspects of your positionality that are relevant to how you might relate to your research question (e.g., your gender, race, types of expertise) and the assumptions and expectations you had. If a prior relationship with the participants exists, you will reflect on how this has influenced your analysis. A prior relationship is not always problematic. It could have aided (e.g., by generating the trust to confide in you) or impaired (e.g., by influencing their honesty or your interpretation) your data collection and analysis or could have done both.

Data Collection

In this section, you will describe your process of data collection and the form of your data (e.g., transcribed interviews, archived data, observation). This will include aspects such as your central questions and the timing, place, and duration of interviews. It also includes the steps you took to manage your perspectives to influence their effect on the data collection (e.g., memoing, researcher reflections, nonleading questions).

Analysis

Because there are many approaches to grounded theory methods, it is useful to detail each step you took. Who conducted each part of the analysis, from creating units, initial categories, higher order categories, and the core category? What procedures did each step entail? If you have a research team, you might describe the training given to prepare members for engaging in interviewing and analysis. Through this description, you will provide rationales (often along with citations) that explain the methodological decisions you have made and tie them to your research goals. I always make clear that my analysis used a bottom-up approach and that my categories resulted from the analysis rather than being developed a priori. It has become typical to indicate the type of software used, if relevant.

Methodological Integrity

There are many ways that qualitative researchers demonstrate that their findings have methodological integrity and show that their claims are warranted (see description of methodological integrity in Chapter 3). When I write grounded theory manuscripts, I include a section on how I have ensured methodological integrity in my study. In this process, I typically emphasize unique features that increased fidelity to my subject matter or how findings were developed to have utility to meet the study goals. These may include checks on methodological integrity such as achieving saturation, memoing, using consensus or auditing, collecting participant feedback, and triangulating findings—that is, assessing the convergence of findings across methods or research teams. I find that organizing this material into a distinct section is helpful because then reviewers who are not as familiar with qualitative research can identify these procedures as functioning to improve the study's integrity.

RESULTS

The Results section is invariably the longest in a grounded theory manuscript. Within a 35-page manuscript, it usually ranges between 10 to 15 pages. Because the expected length of the manuscript is based on the length of quantitative manuscripts, there may be pragmatic issues of a page-length limitation to consider. (See Chapter 4 on the consideration of the numbers of higher order clusters and categories that fit within a manuscript.)

Geertz (1973) described the need for "thick description" to support qualitative research. In the Results section, you will want to be sure to contextualize your findings so that readers understand when, where, and under what conditions they were found to hold. Also, you will want to bring your results to life by using evocative quotations, exemplars, and details that allow your readers to bring a range of associations to bear on the reading of your findings.

At the beginning of the Results section, it is typical to have a paragraph that describes the hierarchy, including the number of meaning units created, the number of levels in the hierarchy, and the number of clusters and categories under the core category, to orient the reader to the form of the findings you will be presenting. If you present the number of participants whose meaning units contributed to your categories and cluster, this paragraph also should describe how to interpret those numbers. I usually include a sentence to indicate that these numbers cannot be interpreted as indicating agreement on a finding when the interviews are semistructured because different questions may have been asked to each participant. Also, participants may have agreed with an idea but simply did not think to mention it, worried about being judged for the idea, or thought it was understood already. There are many reasons an idea can be omitted.

Instead, I clarify that these numbers can be used as an indicator of how salient the ideas were for the participants at the time of the interview (Levitt, 2015). Salience may increase when an idea is centrally important and when an experience is more present in the dominant discourses related to a topic (e.g., #MeToo) or because of events occurring near the time of the interview (e.g., an election). In contrast, if you are seeking a way to assess the proportion of participants who agree with a finding, seeking feedback from them on the findings can be the best way to do this. In this first paragraph, you also may refer readers to an overview table that presents the core category, clusters, and categories that comprise your results. Often, I will list the number of participants whose data contributed to each in the table as well.

The Results section is structured so that each cluster becomes a major section, with the core category being the concluding section. (It is more efficient to have the core category at the end of the description of the clusters so that readers understand the concepts that the core category is based on when they learn about it.) Usually, I use the cluster labels as the section headings; however, if the journal has formatting restrictions, I will use a shorter version of the cluster label and then present the full label in the first line of each section. If the journal permits enough space to describe the hierarchy adequately, it may be possible to have subsections within each cluster section that describe the categories therein, with headings that present the category title. If the page limits are more restrictive, you may need to describe the categories in a collapsed fashion and describe the cluster. It is unlikely that you will be able to describe any level of the hierarchy beneath the category, but this is okay because those meanings are subsumed in the categories, and they are represented in that manner.

Within the subsection for each cluster, I usually describe the concept of the cluster briefly and the number of categories it contains to orient the reader. Then, each paragraph in the subsection is based on describing a category therein. Usually, each paragraph includes a sentence that describes that category concept, an illustrative quotation, and finally, a sentence that ties the meaning within the quotation back to the meaning within the category title. Emphasize the commonalities as well as the differences in your finding to best increase the fidelity and utility of your results. When selecting a quotation, there are several things to keep in mind. A good quotation should (a) bring to life the experience being discussed in a vivid manner, (b) obviously connect to the idea of the category while adding detail to the idea, and (c) not contain many idiosyncratic details that might distract from the meaning being illustrated. For instance, compare the following quotations as illustrations on why prejudicial comments at school are harmful.

> The words were upsetting. Prejudice is harmful. I just couldn't get over that comment. I think it happened about a month ago at least, maybe even more, but it feels more recent than that. I felt upset after it happened.

> After the event, I went home, and I cried. . . . I didn't want to tell my parents because I knew that they would feel badly if they thought I was having trouble at school. I thought about telling my friends, but they would probably keep asking me about it, and that would make it feel worse. I felt really alone and didn't know how to protect myself from it happening again.

Both quotations substantiate the idea that prejudice is harmful, but the second quotation brings to life the emotional and interpersonal effects of prejudice. It helps readers step into the experiential world of the participant and deepens their understanding and so is a better quotation. You can edit longer quotations by using ellipses to show where words were removed. After reviewing the categories, at the end of each cluster, I summarize participant feedback that either affirms or clarifies the meanings within that cluster.

At the end of the Results section, you will have a subsection that describes the core category. It can be useful to describe the concepts therein while referencing the clusters in which those concepts were grounded. In the same manner, the reader will understand how the ideas from your core category developed from your analysis. You also may describe any feedback from participants in a paragraph at the end of that section.

It can be helpful to look at how results are presented in the journals to which you are submitting. A typical section then may be structured as in Exhibit 6.1. This template may be a useful guide for you as you begin writing, but feel free to adapt it to your own study structure and practices.

EXHIBIT 6.1. Results Section Template

Results

Orienting paragraph (its contents are described earlier in the section).

Cluster 1: Label

One to two sentences describing the main concept of the cluster and the number of participants whose data contributed to that cluster, as well as the number of categories within it.

Category 1.1

A sentence description of the meaning within that category. An illustrative quotation from the data. A sentence to tie the meaning in the quotation back to the category title and make clear the connection.

Category 1.2

A sentence description of the meaning within that category. An illustrative quotation from the data. A sentence to tie the meaning in the quotation back to the category title and make clear the connection. [Repeat for all categories.]

   A concluding paragraph with any feedback on that cluster from participants that affirms or clarifies the results presented.

Cluster 2: Label [Repeat the same format as in Cluster 1 and continue.]

Core Category: Label

A few paragraphs describing the core category conceptualization and demonstrating how it is rooted in the prior clusters. A description of any participant feedback.

DISCUSSION

Again, because the results require so much space in a grounded theory study, the Discussion section usually has to be briefer and often is between seven and eight pages in length. Although some qualitative traditions combine their results with their discussion so that their reflection on the literature and practical recommendations are combined with their results, it is more typical to keep these separate within grounded theory reports. In this section, researchers are mostly focused on describing how their findings contribute to the literature or address the aims of their research. Because the core category comes immediately before your discussion, you do not want to restate your results in your discussion section. Instead, you will begin by briefly overviewing the subsections in your discussion.

To organize your discussion, you can consider the main two or three contributions that your findings have made and write a subsection on each one. Within the subsections, consider how your findings support, elaborate, or create alternatives to prior research, citing it conscientiously. When there are differences between your findings and prior research, you will want to consider why that might be. Were the populations, questions, contexts, or methods different? Critical-constructivist qualitative researchers are interested in *praxis*, the practical application of theoretical findings. How does your research help to address social inequities or real-world problems? Your sections should include clear statements of the implications of your research for future research, practice, education, or policy and any recommendations.

It is expected that you will have a section on the strengths and limitations of your study. Here you will consider weaknesses in your research design. Were there types of participants who were not included but would be important for future researchers to explore? Were there weaknesses in the quality of the data, sources, or questions that should be acknowledged? What limits are there to transferability—that is, what do readers need to know to appropriately transfer the findings in your study into their own diverse contexts? In making recommendations for future research, you might consider alternative explanations of your data that might be explored and related ethical dilemmas.

7

SUMMARY AND CONCLUSIONS

In this book, I have presented a critical-constructivist interpretation of grounded theory method, emphasizing the many ways you can tailor research procedures to fit your study question and characteristics. Because there are multiple forms of grounded theory, it will be important for you to be clear about the approach you are using and that it is one approach among many. Knowing that many reviewers are not familiar with qualitative methods, you may need to educate reviewers about any approach that you adopt.

Despite their differences, grounded theory method approaches share a number of distinguishing factors that were explained earlier in this book—constant comparison, the development of a hierarchy, theoretical sampling, saturation, and memoing. Articulating your use of these defining features of grounded theory can help establish your method for reviewers. I hope that one of the central messages that you take from this book, however, is to feel empowered to alter, adopt, or craft procedures that support your exploration. By describing each of the procedures you used and the rationale for your method-related decisions, you can help reviewers appreciate your designs.

This book has provided guidance on how to increase the methodological integrity of your research by considering how each procedure supports the fidelity and utility of your specific study. It also provided guidance on how to

https://doi.org/10.1037/0000231-007
Essentials of Critical-Constructivist Grounded Theory Research, by H. M. Levitt

understand these procedures within a critical-constructivist epistemological framework. I encourage you to flexibly shape research procedures to deepen your inquiry and use the explanations in this book to help you articulate your rationale for adaptations of procedures. The better able you are to demonstrate the fit of your design to your goals, the more confidence your readers and reviewers will have in your findings.

BENEFITS AND ADVANTAGES OF CRITICAL-CONSTRUCTIVIST GROUNDED THEORY

Throughout the book, I have described a wide variety of benefits of using grounded theory methods. These include the ability to develop theory, descriptions of experiences and practices, or interpretations of a phenomenon that are firmly rooted in your data. The formation of a hierarchy has unique advantages for goals such as the development of treatment programs, educational curricula, measures, or policy plans.

I find that it is an excellent initial qualitative method to learn because the clear steps to follow have a straightforward simplicity, and there is room to tailor your methods to your study. Rennie (2000) described this process as a reconciliation of relativism and realism—that is, the interpretive process and the empirical study of data—arguing that this is why grounded theory has such a widespread appeal. It supports researchers in the use of their interpretive skills in such a way that they are faithful to the data undergoing empirical analysis.

LIMITATIONS AND WEAKNESSES OF CRITICAL-CONSTRUCTIVIST GROUNDED THEORY

Grounded theory methods only do what they are meant to do. In Chapter 2, I detailed the circumstances in which a question would be better suited to another form of analysis (if a hierarchy is not necessary, the data are not rich enough to support a hierarchical analysis, or the study aim is focused on a single phenomenon).

The central limitation of the theory is the time that this kind of analysis can take relative to many other qualitative methods. Often, what determines success is researchers' commitment and curiosity, which leads them to appreciate the insights and benefits of this attuned form of analysis. The close analysis of data and the development of a hierarchy occurs over a stretch of time. In my qualitative methods graduate-level course (Levitt et al., 2013), we begin with a research question and are able to jointly develop a rough first draft of a paper by the end of a 15-week semester. It invariably takes longer to have an article ready to submit for publication, however, and I usually recommend at least a year for a thesis or dissertation project (and potentially more if the process of recruitment is expected to be lengthy).

But if you are intrigued by the phenomenon you are studying and driven to understand its workings, it is an absolute pleasure to use grounded theory methods. I remember being told that I would be sick of my dissertation topic by the end of writing it (on the function of silences in psychotherapy; Levitt, 2001), but instead, my grounded theory analysis launched a multistudy program of research, the development of a process measure on in-session silences, and a career's worth of reflection across questions, research teams, and cultures (Levitt & Morrill, in press). I find that the process of structuring a hierarchy never fails to lead me to appreciate an issue more deeply and strengthen my enthusiasm for that issue.

DEVELOPING A THESIS OR DISSERTATION TIMELINE

A rough timeline that can be helpful when developing a grounded theory project or when supervising one is presented in Table 7.1. It flags the moments in the analysis that I find useful for students to check in with an advisor. Checking in with someone who has experience using grounded theory or with the topic you are studying can be helpful to stay on track. Also, you will want to adjust the timeline, given the realities of a project. You may have more or fewer rounds of data collection, for instance, or constraints on your time that require more or less time for data collection or analysis. All your data may need to be collected in one round, for instance, because participants are only available during a certain window (but you can still analyze data in waves). A detailed description of all the activities in Table 7.1 is provided earlier in the text, so at this point, you can consider how long you might want to allot for each step in the analytic process.

This timeline is somewhat conservative, so it can be helpful for you to adjust it as you consider the amount of time you or your students have to allocate to your project each week. In my experience, some students work more quickly than others—it mostly depends on the amount of time they can dedicate to it, given other life constraints. Entering actual dates into your timeline can allow you to account for holidays or times unavailable for work. Also, note that the timeline does not include the time it takes for your university institutional review board to approve your project or for your committee members to review your work.

TABLE 7.1. Example Project Timeline With Three Rounds of Data Collection and Analysis

Weeks (42 total)	Activity	Advisor check
5 weeks	Gather three to four interviews and transcribe them (ideally, transcribe the same day as the interviews).	Meet with your advisor with the first transcribed interview to review for feedback until your interviewing skills are approved.
2 weeks	Create meaning units for three to four transcripts.	Meet with your advisor with the first unitized interview to review for feedback until your unitizing and labeling skills are approved.
3 weeks	Use constant comparison to organize the initial categories of the hierarchy based on the first three to four transcripts. Consider whether there is anything missing in the interview findings that might direct future recruiting (see theoretical sampling).	Meet with your advisor to review the categorizing process and labeling of initial categories. Discuss sampling.
3 weeks	Create the next level of higher order categories in the hierarchy for three to four transcripts. Begin to recruit for the second round of interviews.	Meet with your advisor to review the categorizing process and labeling of higher order categories.
2 weeks	Form the cluster levels and tighten the hierarchy so there are no more than eight clusters at the highest level, and all lower level categories are subsumed.	Meet with your advisor to review the categorizing process and labeling of higher order categories.
2 weeks	Gather a second round of data and transcribe—about four to five more interviews.	Meet with your advisor and continue to refine higher order categories. Discuss new emerging themes.
2 weeks	Create meaning units for the second round of interviews.	Discuss the development of the hierarchy with your advisor.
3 weeks	Use constant comparison to enter the second round of units into the hierarchy. Consider any gaps in your evolving theory with regard to recruitment (theoretical sampling).	Discuss the development of the hierarchy with your advisor. Discuss sampling.
2 weeks	Conduct a hierarchy review to refine the analysis and prepare for tracking saturation. Begin to recruit for the third round of interviews.	It can help if your advisor can conduct an independent hierarchy review as well and provide feedback.

(continues)

TABLE 7.1. Example Project Timeline With Three Rounds of Data Collection and Analysis (*Continued*)

Weeks (42 total)	Activity	Advisor check
2 weeks	Gather the third round of data and transcribe—approximately four to five more interviews, but track for saturation to guide this number.	Meet with advisor and continue to refine higher order categories. Discuss new emerging themes.
2 weeks	Create meaning units for the third round of interviews.	Discuss the development of the hierarchy with your advisor.
3 weeks	Use constant comparison to enter second round of units into the hierarchy. Consider any gaps in your evolving theory with regard to recruitment (theoretical sampling).	Discuss the development of the hierarchy with your advisor. Discuss sampling.
3 weeks	Write results and send letters to solicit feedback from participants, if desired.	Review feedback letter with your advisor and seek feedback on how intelligible the summary of results is. Discuss the process of writing results.
2 weeks	Write discussion while your advisor reviews your results. Send feedback letters, if desired.	Discuss the process of writing the discussion.
2 weeks	Revise results while your advisor reviews your discussion. Integrate feedback into your results.	Discuss feedback on results.
2 weeks	Revise the discussion. Revise the introduction and method (change tense and add in details on participants).	Discuss feedback on the discussion. Possibly consider journals to submit your work.
2 weeks	Begin to draft journal submission while your advisor reviews final changes on your thesis or dissertation.	Discuss final edits.
2 weeks	Submit the final draft to your committee. Continue to work on the journal submission.	Discuss the journal submission.

FINAL THOUGHTS

Reading other grounded theory research will help you develop a sense of how these methods are enacted within psychology. Like all qualitative methods, the successful adoption of grounded theory methods largely depends on tailoring your method with an eye toward the specific research aims and the study characteristics. This book has guided you through many rationales for and forms of adaptation of grounded theory procedures so that they can fit your study and goals. My final word of advice is to reflect deeply on the characteristics of your topic, your participants, and the goals for your study. Take the time to consider what would help you to gather data that will reflect the nature of your topic. Take the time to consider what would allow you to draw out the patterns that you see. Grounded theory is a scaffold that can support you to develop a deep and rich understanding. Make it your own.

EXEMPLAR STUDIES

Arczynski, A. V., & Morrow, S. L. (2017). The complexities of power in feminist multicultural psychotherapy supervision. *Journal of Counseling Psychology*, *64*(2), 192–205. https://doi.org/10.1037/cou0000179

Bowleg, L. (2004). Love, sex, and masculinity in sociocultural context: HIV concerns and condom use among African American men in heterosexual relationships. *Men and Masculinities*, *7*(2), 166–186. https://doi.org/10.1177/1097184X03257523

Granek, L., Nakash, O., Ariad, S., Shapira, S., & Ben-David, M. (2019). Cancer patients' mental health distress and suicidality: Impact on oncology health-care workers and coping strategies. *Crisis*, *40*, 429–436. https://doi.org/10.1027/0227-5910/a000591

Jacobson, C. H., Zlatnik, M. G., Kennedy, H. P., & Lyndon, A. (2013). Nurses' perspectives on the intersection of safety and informed decision making in maternity care. *Journal of Obstetric, Gynecologic, & Neonatal Nursing*, *42*(5), 577–587. https://doi.org/10.1111/1552-6909.12232
[Exemplar of situational analysis]

Levitt, H. M., Pomerville, A., & Surace, F. I. (2016). A qualitative meta-analysis examining clients' experiences of psychotherapy: A new agenda. *Psychological Bulletin*, *142*(8), 801–830. https://doi.org/10.1037/bul0000057
[Exemplar of meta-analysis using grounded theory methods]

Oddli, H. W., Kjøs, P., & McLeod, J. (2017). Negotiating credibility: The peer review process in clinical research. *Qualitative Psychology*, *7*(1), 59–75. https://doi.org/10.1037/qup0000114

Rihacek, T., & Danelova, E. (2016). The journey of an integrationist: A grounded theory analysis. *Psychotherapy*, *53*(1), 78–89. https://doi.org/10.1037/pst0000040

References

Age, L. (2011). Grounded theory methodology: Positivism, hermeneutics, and pragmatism. *Qualitative Report, 16*(6), 1599–1615.

Allen, M. (2011). Violence and voice: Using a feminist constructivist grounded theory to explore women's resistance to abuse. *Qualitative Research, 11*(1), 23–45. https://doi.org/10.1177/1468794110384452

American Psychological Association. (2017). *Ethical principles of psychologists and code of conduct* (2002, amended effective June 1, 2010, and January 1, 2017). https://www.apa.org/ethics/code/index.aspx

American Psychological Association. (2020). *Publication manual of the American Psychological Association* (7th ed.). https://doi.org/10.1037/0000165-000

Arczynski, A. V., Christensen, M. C., & Hoover, S. M. (2018). Fostering critical feminist multicultural qualitative research mentoring. *The Counseling Psychologist, 46*(8), 954–978. https://doi.org/10.1177/0011000018823782

Arczynski, A. V., & Morrow, S. L. (2017). The complexities of power in feminist multicultural psychotherapy supervision. *Journal of Counseling Psychology.* Advance online publication. https://doi.org/10.1037/cou0000179

Auerbach, C. F., Salick, E., & Fine, J. (2006). Using grounded theory to develop treatment strategies for multicontextual trauma. *Professional Psychology, Research and Practice, 37*(4), 367–373. https://doi.org/10.1037/0735-7028.37.4.367

Bemak, F., & Chung, R. C. Y. (2017). Refugee trauma: Culturally responsive counseling interventions. *Journal of Counseling and Development, 95*(3), 299–308. https://doi.org/10.1002/jcad.12144

Bettez, S. C. (2015). Navigating the complexity of qualitative research in postmodern contexts: Assemblage, critical reflexivity, and communion as guides. *International Journal of Qualitative Studies in Education, 28*(8), 932–954. https://doi.org/10.1080/09518398.2014.948096

Bowleg, L. (2004). Love, sex, and masculinity in sociocultural context: HIV concerns and condom use among African American men in heterosexual relationships. *Men and Masculinities, 7*(2), 166–186. https://doi.org/10.1177/1097184X03257523

Braun, V., & Clarke, V. (2019). To saturate or not to saturate? Questioning data saturation as a useful concept for thematic analysis and sample-size rationales. *Qualitative Research in Sport, Exercise and Health.* Advance online publication. https://doi.org/10.1080/2159676X.2019.1704846

Bryant, A., & Charmaz, K. (2013). Grounded theory in historical perspective: An epistemological account. In A. Bryant & K. Charmaz (Eds.), *The SAGE handbook of grounded theory* (pp. 31–57). SAGE.

Buckley, C. A., & Waring, M. J. (2013). Using diagrams to support the research process: Examples from grounded theory. *Qualitative Research, 13*(2), 148–172. https://doi.org/10.1177/1468794112472280

Budge, S. L., Belcourt, S., Conniff, J., Parks, R., Pantalone, D., & Katz-Wise, S. L. (2018). A grounded theory study of the development of trans youths' awareness of coping with gender identity. *Journal of Child and Family Studies.* Advance online publication. https://doi.org/10.1007/s10826-018-1136-y

Burman, E. (2006). Emotions and reflexivity in feminised education action research. *Educational Action Research, 14*(3), 315–332. https://doi.org/10.1080/09650790600847636

Carrero, V., Peiró, J. M., & Salanova, M. (2000). Studying radical organizational innovation through grounded theory. *European Journal of Work and Organizational Psychology, 9*(4), 489–514. https://doi.org/10.1080/13594320050203102

Cartwright, N. (2007). *Hunting causes and using them.* Cambridge University Press. https://doi.org/10.1017/CBO9780511618758

Castillo, L. G., Brossart, D. F., Reyes, C. J., Conoley, C. W., & Phoummarath, M. J. (2007). The influence of multicultural training on perceived multicultural counseling competencies and implicit racial prejudice. *Journal of Multicultural Counseling and Development, 35*(4), 243–255. https://doi.org/10.1002/j.2161-1912.2007.tb00064.x

Chang, D. F., & Yoon, P. (2011). Ethnic minority clients' perceptions of the significance of race in cross-racial therapy relationships. *Psychotherapy Research, 21,* 567–582. https://doi.org/10.1080/10503307.2011.592549

Charmaz, K. (2008). Constructionism and the grounded theory. In J. A. Holstein & J. F. Gubrium (Eds.), *Handbook of constructionist research* (pp. 397–412). Guilford Press.

Charmaz, K. (2014). *Constructing grounded theory* (2nd ed.). SAGE.

Clarke, A. E. (2003). Situational analyses: Grounded theory mapping after the postmodern turn. *Symbolic Interaction, 26*(4), 553–576. https://doi.org/10.1525/si.2003.26.4.553

Clarke, A. E. (2009). From grounded theory to situational analysis: What's new? Why? How? In J. M. Morse, P. N. Stern, J. Corbin, B. Bowers, K. Charmaz, & A. E. Clarke (Eds.), *Developing grounded theory: The second generation* (pp. 194–233). Left Coast Press.

Code, L. (1993). Taking subjectivity into account. In L. Alcoff & E. Potter (Eds.), *Feminist epistemologies* (pp. 23–57). Routledge.

Corbin, J. M. (1998). Alternative explanations: Valid or not? *Theory & Psychology, 8*(1), 121–128. https://doi.org/10.1177/0959354398081007

Creswell, J. W. (2009). *Research design: Qualitative, quantitative, and mixed methods approaches* (3rd ed.). SAGE.

Diamond, L. M. (2006). Careful what you ask for: Reconsidering feminist epistemology and autobiographical narrative in research on sexual identity development. *Signs: Journal of Women in Culture and Society, 31*(2), 471–491. https://doi.org/10.1086/491684

Elliott, R., Fischer, C. T., & Rennie, D. L. (1999). Evolving guidelines for publication of qualitative research studies in psychology and related fields. *British Journal of Clinical Psychology, 38*, 215–229. https://doi.org/10.1348/014466599162782

Ellis, B. H., Kia-Keating, M., Yusuf, S. A., Lincoln, A., & Nur, A. (2007). Ethical research in refugee communities and the use of community participatory methods. *Transcultural Psychiatry, 44*, 459–481. https://doi.org/10.1177/1363461507081642

Fassinger, R. E. (2005). Paradigms, praxis, problems, and promise: Grounded theory in counseling psychology research. *Journal of Counseling Psychology, 52*(2), 156–166. https://doi.org/10.1037/0022-0167.52.2.156

Fine, M. (2013). Echoes of Bedford: A 20-year social psychology memoir on participatory action research hatched behind bars. *American Psychologist, 68*(8), 687–698. https://doi.org/10.1037/a0034359

Fine, M. (2016). Just methods in revolting times. *Qualitative Research in Psychology, 13*(4), 347–365. https://doi.org/10.1080/14780887.2016.1219800

Fishman, D. B., & Westerman, M. A. (2011). A key role for case studies: Theory building. *Pragmatic Case Studies in Psychotherapy, 7*(4), 434–439. https://doi.org/10.14713/pcsp.v7i4.1111

Flyvbjerg, B. (2006). Five misunderstandings about case-study research. *Qualitative Inquiry, 12*(2), 219–245. https://doi.org/10.1177/1077800405284363

Foss, S. K., & Foss, K. A. (2011). *Inviting transformation: Presentational speaking for a changing world* (3rd ed.). Waveland.

Fox, D., & Prilleltensky, I. (Eds.). (1997). *Critical psychology: An introduction.* SAGE.

Freud, S. (1900). *The interpretation of dreams.* Norton.

Geertz, C. (1973). *Thick description: Toward an interpretive theory of culture.* Basic Books.

Gibson, B. (2013). Accommodating critical theory. In A. Bryant & K. Charmaz (Eds.), *The SAGE handbook of grounded theory* (pp. 436–453). SAGE.

Giorgi, A. (2009). *The descriptive phenomenological method in psychology: A modified Husserlian approach.* Duquesne University Press.

Glaser, B. G. (1992). *Emergence vs forcing: The basics of grounded theory analysis.* Sociology Press.

Glaser, B. G. (1998). *Doing grounded theory: Issues and discussions*. Sociology Press.

Glaser, B. G. (2013). Doing formal grounded theory. In A. Bryant & K. Charmaz (Eds.), *The SAGE handbook of grounded theory* (pp. 96–114). SAGE.

Glaser, B. G., & Strauss, A. L. (1967). *The discovery of grounded theory: Strategies for qualitative research*. Aldine.

Gone, J. P. (2019). "The thing happened as he wished": Recovering an American Indian cultural psychology. *American Journal of Community Psychology*, *64*(1–2), 172–184. https://doi.org/10.1002/ajcp.12353

Gough, B., & Lyons, A. (2016). The future of qualitative research in psychology: Accentuating the positive. *Integrative Psychological & Behavioral Science*, *50*(2), 234–243. https://doi.org/10.1007/s12124-015-9320-8

Granek, L., Nakash, O., Ariad, S., Shapira, S., & Ben, D. M. A. (2019). Oncology health care professionals' perspectives on the causes of mental health distress in cancer patients. *Psycho-Oncology*, *28*(8), 1695–1701. https://doi.org/10.1002/pon.5144

Grzanka, P. R. (2020). The shape of knowledge: Situational analysis in counseling psychology research. *Journal of Counseling Psychology*. Advance online publication. https://doi.org/10.1037/cou0000527

Guba, E. G., & Lincoln, Y. S. (2005). Paradigmatic controversies, contradictions, and emerging confluences. In N. K. Denzin & Y. S. Lincoln (Eds.), *The SAGE handbook of qualitative research* (pp. 191–215). SAGE.

Harding, S. (2015). *Objectivity and diversity: Another logic of scientific research*. University of Chicago Press. https://doi.org/10.7208/chicago/9780226241531.001.0001

Heath, H., & Cowley, S. (2004). Developing a grounded theory approach: A comparison of Glaser and Strauss. *International Journal of Nursing Studies*, *41*(2), 141–150. https://doi.org/10.1016/S0020-7489(03)00113-5

Hill, C. E. (2012). *Consensual qualitative research: A practical resource for investigating social science phenomena*. American Psychological Association.

Jacobson, C. H., Zlatnik, M. G., Kennedy, H. P., & Lyndon, A. (2013). Nurses' perspectives on the intersection of safety and informed decision making in maternity care. *Journal of Obstetric, Gynecologic, & Neonatal Nursing*, *42*(5), 577–587. https://doi.org/10.1111/1552-6909.12232

Jeon, Y.-H. (2004). The application of grounded theory and symbolic interactionism. *Scandinavian Journal of Caring Sciences*, *18*(3), 249–256. https://doi.org/10.1111/j.1471-6712.2004.00287.x

Josselson, R. (2013). *Interviewing for qualitative inquiry: A relational approach*. Guilford Press.

Kafer, A. (2013). *Feminist queer crip*. Indiana University Press.

Kearney, M. H. (2001). Enduring love: A grounded formal theory of women's experience of domestic violence. *Research in Nursing & Health*, *24*(4), 270–282. https://doi.org/10.1002/nur.1029

Kempster, S., & Parry, K. W. (2011). Grounded theory and leadership research: A critical realist perspective. *The Leadership Quarterly, 22*(1), 106–120. https://doi.org/10.1016/j.leaqua.2010.12.010

Levitt, H. M. (1999). The development of wisdom: An analysis of Tibetan Buddhist experience. *Journal of Humanistic Psychology, 39*(2), 86–105. https://doi.org/10.1177/0022167899392006

Levitt, H. M. (2001). Sounds of silence in psychotherapy: The categorization of clients' pauses. *Psychotherapy Research, 11*(3), 295–309. https://doi.org/10.1080/713663985

Levitt, H. M. (2015). Interpretation-driven guidelines for designing and evaluating grounded theory research: A constructivist-social justice approach. In O. Gelo, A. Pritz, & B. Rieken (Eds.), *Psychotherapy research: Foundations, outcome and process* (pp. 455–483). Springer. https://doi.org/10.1007/978-3-7091-1382-0_22

Levitt, H. M. (2019). A psychosocial genealogy of LGBTQ+ gender: An empirically based theory of gender and gender identity cultures. *Psychology of Women Quarterly, 43*(3), 275–297. https://doi.org/10.1177/0361684319834641

Levitt, H. M. (in press). Qualitative generalization, not to the population but to the phenomenon: A reconceptualization of variation in qualitative research. *Qualitative Psychology.*

Levitt, H. M., Bamberg, M., Creswell, J. W., Frost, D. M., Josselson, R., & Suárez-Orozco, C. (2018). Journal article reporting standards for qualitative primary, qualitative meta-analytic, and mixed methods research in psychology: The APA Publications and Communications Board Task Force report. *American Psychologist, 73*(1), 26–46. https://doi.org/10.1037/amp0000151

Levitt, H. M., & Hiestand, K. R. (2004). A quest for authenticity: Contemporary butch gender. *Sex Roles, 50*, 605–621. https://doi.org/10.1023/B:SERS.0000027565.59109.80

Levitt, H. M., Ipecki, B., Morrill, Z., & Rizo, J. (2020). *Do we have consensus on consensus?* [Manuscript submitted for publication]. Department of Psychology, University of Massachusetts Boston.

Levitt, H. M., & Ippolito, M. R. (2014). Being transgender: Navigating minority stressors and developing authentic self-presentation. *Psychology of Women Quarterly, 38*, 46–64. https://doi.org/10.1177/0361684313501644

Levitt, H. M., Ippolito, M. R., & Kannan, D. (2013). Teaching qualitative methods using a research team approach: Publishing grounded theory projects with your class. *Qualitative Research in Psychology, 10*(2), 119–139. https://doi.org/10.1080/14780887.2011.586101

Levitt, H. M., & Morrill, Z. (in press). Measuring silence: The pausing inventory categorization system and a review of findings. In M. Buchholz & A. Dimitrijevic (Eds.), *Silence and silencing in psychoanalysis: Cultural, clinical and research perspectives*. Routledge.

Levitt, H. M., Morrill, Z., Collins, K. M., & Rizo, J. (in press). The methodological integrity of critical qualitative research: Principles to support design and research review. *Journal of Counseling Psychology*.

Levitt, H. M., Motulsky, S. L., Wertz, F. J., Morrow, S. L., & Ponterotto, J. G. (2017). Recommendations for designing and reviewing qualitative research in psychology: Promoting methodological integrity. *Qualitative Psychology*, *4*(1), 2–22. https://doi.org/10.1037/qup0000082

Levitt, H. M., Pomerville, A., & Surace, F. I. (2016). A qualitative meta-analysis examining clients' experiences of psychotherapy: A new agenda. *Psychological Bulletin*. Advance online publication. https://doi.org/10.1037/bul0000057

Levitt, H. M., Pomerville, A., Surace, F. I., & Grabowski, L. M. (2017). Meta-method study of qualitative psychotherapy research on clients' experiences: Review and recommendations. *Journal of Counseling Psychology*, *64*, 626–644. https://doi.org/10.1037/cou0000222

Levitt, H. M., Surace, F. I., Wu, M. B., Chapin, B., Hargrove, J. G., Herbitter, C., Lu, E. C., Maroney, M. R., & Hochman, A. L. (in press). The meaning of scientific objectivity and subjectivity: From the perspective of methodologists. *Psychological Methods*.

Levitt, H. M., & Ware, K. (2006). "Anything with two heads is a monster": Religious leaders' perspectives on marital equality and domestic violence. *Violence Against Women*, *12*(12), 1169–1190. https://doi.org/10.1177/1077801206293546

Levitt, H. M., & Williams, D. C. (2010). Facilitating client change: Principles based upon the experience of eminent psychotherapists. *Psychotherapy Research*, *20*(3), 337–352. https://doi.org/10.1080/10503300903476708

Lincoln, Y. S., & Guba, E. G. (1985). *Naturalistic inquiry*. SAGE. https://doi.org/10.1016/0147-1767(85)90062-8

Lindlof, T. R., & Taylor, B. C. (2017). *Qualitative communication research methods* (4th ed.). SAGE.

Lo, C. O. (2014). Enhancing groundedness in realist grounded theory research. *Qualitative Psychology*, *1*(1), 61–76. https://doi.org/10.1037/qup0000001

Madill, A. (2015). Let a thousand flowers bloom. *The Psychologist*, *28*(8), 656–658. https://thepsychologist.bps.org.uk/volume-28/august-2015/let-thousand-flowers-bloom

Maslow, A. H. (1968). *Toward a psychology of being*. Van Nostrand Reinhold.

Maxwell, J. A. (2012). The importance of qualitative research for causal explanation in education. *Qualitative Inquiry*, *18*(8), 655–661. https://doi.org/10.1177/1077800412452856

McEvoy, B. (2019). *The experiences of mothers who have a child diagnosed with cancer* [Unpublished doctoral dissertation]. Trinity College, University of Dublin.

Moradi, B., & Grzanka, P. R. (2017). Using intersectionality responsibly: Toward critical epistemology, structural analysis, and social justice activism. *Journal of Counseling Psychology*, *64*(5), 500–513. https://doi.org/10.1037/cou0000203

Morawski, J. G. (2005). Reflexivity and the psychologist. *History of the Human Sciences*, *18*(4), 77–105. https://doi.org/10.1177/0952695105058472

Morrow, S. L. (2005). Quality and trustworthiness in qualitative research in counseling psychology. *Journal of Counseling Psychology, 52*(2), 250–260. https://doi.org/10.1037/0022-0167.52.2.250

Motulsky, S. L. (2019, June 10–11). Is member checking the gold standard of quality within qualitative research? In R. Tuval-Mashiach (Chair), *Questioning qualitative methods* [Symposium]. Society for Qualitative Inquiry in Psychology Annual Conference on Qualitative Research Methods, Boston, MA.

Oddli, H. W., Kjøs, P., & McLeod, J. (2017). Negotiating credibility: The peer review process in clinical research. *Qualitative Psychology, 7*(1), 59–75. https://doi.org/10.1037/qup0000114

Oddli, H. W., & Rønnestad, M. H. (2012). How experienced therapists introduce the technical aspects in the initial alliance formation: Powerful decision makers supporting clients' agency. *Psychotherapy Research, 22*(2), 176–193. https://doi.org/10.1080/10503307.2011.633280

Olsen, V. L. (2013). Feminist qualitative research and grounded theory: Complexities, criticisms and opportunities. In A. Bryant & K. Charmaz (Eds.), *The SAGE handbook of grounded theory* (pp. 417–435). SAGE.

Osbeck, L. M. (2014). Scientific reasoning as sense making: Implications for qualitative inquiry. *Qualitative Psychology, 1*(1), 34–46. https://doi.org/10.1037/qup0000004

Parker, I. (Ed.). (2015). *Handbook of critical psychology*. Routledge/Taylor & Francis.

Patton, M. J. (2015). *Qualitative research and evaluation methods: Integrating theory and practice* (4th ed.). SAGE.

Ponterotto, J. G. (2005). Qualitative research in counseling psychology: A primer on research paradigms and philosophy of science. *Journal of Counseling Psychology, 52*(2), 126–136. https://doi.org/10.1037/0022-0167.52.2.126

Rennie, D. L. (1998). Grounded theory methodology: The pressing need for a logic of justification. *Theory & Psychology, 8*(1), 101–119. https://doi.org/10.1177/0959354398081006

Rennie, D. L. (2000). Grounded theory methodology as methodical hermeneutics: Reconciling realism and relativism. *Theory & Psychology, 10*(4), 481–502. https://doi.org/10.1177/0959354300104003

Rennie, D. L. (2007). Reflexivity and its radical form: Implications for the practice of humanistic psychotherapies. *Journal of Contemporary Psychotherapy, 37*(1), 53–58. https://doi.org/10.1007/s10879-006-9035-8

Rennie, D. L. (2010). Humanistic psychology at York University: Retrospective: Focus on clients' experiencing in psychotherapy: Emphasis of radical reflexivity. *The Humanistic Psychologist, 38*(1), 40–56. https://doi.org/10.1080/08873261003635856

Rennie, D. L. (2012). Qualitative research as methodical hermeneutics. *Psychological Methods, 17*, 385–398. https://doi.org/10.1037/a0029250

Rennie, D. L., & Fergus, K. D. (2006). Embodied categorizing in the grounded theory method: Methodical hermeneutics in action. *Theory & Psychology, 16*(4), 483–503. https://doi.org/10.1177/0959354306066202

Rennie, D. L., Phillips, J. R., & Quartaro, G. K. (1988). Grounded theory: A promising approach to conceptualization in psychology? *Canadian Psychology, 29*(2), 139–150. https://doi.org/10.1037/h0079765

Rihacek, T., & Danelova, E. (2016). The journey of an integrationist: A grounded theory analysis. *Psychotherapy, 53*(1), 78–89. https://doi.org/10.1037/pst0000040

Roberts, J. M. (2014). Critical realism, dialectics, and qualitative research methods. *Journal for the Theory of Social Behaviour, 44*(1), 1–23. https://doi.org/10.1111/jtsb.12056

Shelton, K., & Delgado-Romero, E. A. (2013). Sexual orientation microaggressions: The experience of lesbian, gay, bisexual, and queer clients in psychotherapy. *Psychology of Sexual Orientation and Gender Diversity, 1*(S), 59–70. https://doi.org/10.1037/2329-0382.1.S.59

Steinberg, S. R., & Cannella, G. S. (2012). *Critical qualitative research reader.* Peter Lang.

Strauss, A., & Corbin, J. (1990). *Basics of qualitative research: Grounded theory procedures and techniques.* SAGE.

Strauss, A., & Corbin, J. (1998). *Basics of qualitative research: Techniques and procedures for developing grounded theory* (2nd ed.). SAGE.

Sutcliffe, A. (2016). Grounded theory: A method for practitioner research by educational psychologists. *Educational and Child Psychology, 33*(3), 44–54.

Teo, T. (2015). Critical psychology: A geography of intellectual engagement and resistance. *American Psychologist, 70*(3), 243–254. https://doi.org/10.1037/a0038727

Tiefer, L. (2018). More about sexualities activisms please, we need it! *Sexualities, 21*(8), 1246–1250. https://doi.org/10.1177/1363460718770449

Timulak, L. (2009). Meta-analysis of qualitative studies: A tool for reviewing qualitative research findings in psychotherapy. *Psychotherapy Research, 19*(4–5), 591–600. https://doi.org/10.1080/10503300802477989

Timulak, L., & Elliott, R. (2018). Taking stock of descriptive–interpretative qualitative psychotherapy research: Issues and observations from the front line. *Counselling & Psychotherapy Research.* Advance online publication. https://doi.org/10.1002/capr.12197

Tuck, E., & Yang, K. W. (2014). R-words: Refusing research. In D. Paris & M. T. Winn (Eds.), *Humanizing research: Decolonizing qualitative inquiry with youth and communities* (pp. 223–248). SAGE. https://doi.org/10.4135/9781544329611.n12

Tuhiwai Smith, L. (2012). *Decolonizing methodologies: Research and indigenous peoples.* Zed Books.

Tuval-Mashiach, R. (2020). *Is replication important for qualitative researchers?* [Manuscript submitted for publication]. Psychology and Gender Studies, Bar-Ilan University.

Wertz, F. J. (2014). Qualitative inquiry in the history of psychology. *Qualitative Psychology, 1*(1), 4–16. https://doi.org/10.1037/qup0000007

Woods, M., Paulus, T., Atkins, D. P., & Macklin, R. (2016). Advancing qualitative research using qualitative data analysis software (QDAS)? Reviewing potential versus practice in published studies using ATLASti and NVivo, 1994–2013. *Social Science Computer Review, 34*(5), 597–617. https://doi.org/10.1177/0894439315596311

Zavella, P. (1993). Feminist insider dilemmas: Constructing ethnic identity with "Chicana" informants. *Frontiers, 13*(3), 53–70. https://doi.org/10.2307/3346743

Index

About the Author

Heidi M. Levitt, PhD, is a professor in the Clinical Psychology program at the University of Massachusetts Boston. She is a past president of the Society for Qualitative Inquiry in Psychology (SQIP), a section of Division 5 (Quantitative and Qualitative Methods) of the American Psychological Association (APA). In addition, she has been an associate editor for the journals *Psychotherapy Research* and *Qualitative Psychology*. She chaired the development of the SQIP recommendations for reviewing and designing qualitative research (Levitt et al., 2017); chaired the development of the inaugural APA journal article reporting standards (JARS) for qualitative, qualitative meta-analytic, and mixed methods research; and advised on their integration into the seventh edition of the *Publication Manual of the American Psychological Association* (2020). Her research has focused on psychotherapy processes and outcomes and LGBTQ+ genders and communities. She has been awarded fellow status by APA via Divisions 5, 29 (Society for the Advancement of Psychotherapy), 32 (Society for Humanistic Psychology), and 44 (Society for the Psychology of Sexual Orientation and Gender Diversity). Dr. Levitt is a recipient of the APA Division 5 Distinguished Contributions in Qualitative Inquiry Award.

About the Series Editors

Clara E. Hill, PhD, earned her doctorate at Southern Illinois University in 1974. She started her career in 1974 as an assistant professor in the Department of Psychology, University of Maryland, College Park, and is currently there as a professor.

She is the president-elect of the Society for the Advancement of Psychotherapy, and has been the president of the Society for Psychotherapy Research, the editor of the *Journal of Counseling Psychology*, and the editor of *Psychotherapy Research*.

Dr. Hill was awarded the Leona Tyler Award for Lifetime Achievement in Counseling Psychology from Division 17 (Society of Counseling Psychology) and the Distinguished Psychologist Award from Division 29 (Society for the Advancement of Psychotherapy) of the American Psychological Association, the Distinguished Research Career Award from the Society for Psychotherapy Research, and the Outstanding Lifetime Achievement Award from the Section on Counseling and Psychotherapy Process and Outcome Research of the Society for Counseling Psychology. Her major research interests are helping skills, psychotherapy process and outcome, training therapists, dream work, and qualitative research.

She has published more than 250 journal articles, 80 chapters in books, and 17 books (including *Therapist Techniques and Client Outcomes: Eight Cases of Brief Psychotherapy*; *Helping Skills: Facilitating Exploration, Insight, and Action*; and *Dream Work in Therapy: Facilitating Exploration, Insight, and Action*).

Sarah Knox, PhD, joined the faculty of Marquette University in 1999 and is a professor in the Department of Counselor Education and Counseling Psychology in the College of Education. She earned her doctorate at the University of Maryland and completed her predoctoral internship at The Ohio State University.

Dr. Knox's research has been published in a number of journals, including *The Counseling Psychologist, Counselling Psychology Quarterly, Journal of Counseling Psychology, Psychotherapy, Psychotherapy Research,* and *Training and Education in Professional Psychology.* Her publications focus on the psychotherapy process and relationship, supervision and training, and qualitative research. She has presented her research both nationally and internationally and has provided workshops on consensual qualitative research at both U.S. and international venues.

She currently serves as coeditor-in-chief of *Counselling Psychology Quarterly* and is also on the publication board of Division 29 (Society for the Advancement of Psychotherapy) of the American Psychological Association. Dr. Knox is a fellow of Division 17 (Society of Counseling Psychology) and Division 29 (Society for the Advancement of Psychotherapy) of the American Psychological Association.